Y0-AGK-155

Knockout Blocks and Sampler Quilts

Judy Martin

CROSLEY-GRIFFITH
PUBLISHING COMPANY, INC.
Grinnell, Iowa

Acknowledgments

The contents and presentation of this book were shaped with input from many quilters and friends. For their opinions and feedback, I wish to thank Barb Lucas, Terri Kirchner, Jeanne Allen, Chris Davies, Connie Doern, Kate Hardy, Mardell Christian, Mary Covert, Liz Forney, Kris Gerhard, Cindy Maruth, Jo Mostrom, Lori Peake, Beth Repp-Danis, Marcella Richardson, Cathy Sanders, Linda Snavely, Jan Stole, and members of the Jewel Box Quilters Guild.

Special thanks to Steve Bennett, Chris Hulin, Linda Medhus, and Margy Sieck for their keen eyes and sharp minds in proofreading this book.

ISBN 0-929589-10-6
Published by Crosley-Griffith
Publishing Company, Inc.
P.O. Box 512
Grinnell, IA 50112
(641) 236-4854
toll free in U.S. (800) 642-5615
e-mail: info@judymartin.com
web site: www.judymartin.com

Printed in U.S.A. by
Acme Printing
Des Moines, Iowa

Exquisite Stars Sampler quilt in twin size (page 16)

Judy Martin encourages the use of this book for kits and classes. Shops and teachers have permission to use the blocks for a Block-of-the-Month series; to use the quilts in project classes or fabric kits; teachers are free to use their own methods and handouts; in any case, each student is required to own *Knockout Blocks & Sampler Quilts.*

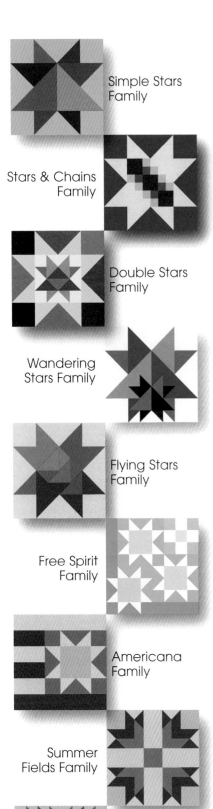

Simple Stars Family

Stars & Chains Family

Double Stars Family

Wandering Stars Family

Flying Stars Family

Free Spirit Family

Americana Family

Summer Fields Family

Shimmering Stars Family

Exquisite Stars Family

Contents

Introduction

Knockout Blocks and Sampler Quilts is three books rolled into one. It is a block resource, a quilt pattern book, and a quilt planning reference with charts for yardage, quilt sizes, and so on. These elements all come into play as I explore block families and how to use them. I use related blocks to make a new kind of sampler quilt. I also illustrate numerous non-sampler quilts for which you may substitute other blocks from the same family. The book aims to please the intermediate quilter, but it is also ideal for beginners in a classroom setting.

When I began work on the book, I intended it to be a compilation of readers' favorite patterns reprinted from a series that ran on my website. However, I am just not one to rehash old material, and the book soon took a different turn.

Not Your Same Old Blocks

By the end, only ten of 109 blocks came from my Block-of-the-Moment patterns online. Six of the 47 quilts shown were developed from setting suggestions in those patterns. Eleven blocks are basic traditional ones that are good mixers. The remaining 88 blocks and 41 quilts are completely new. Even the format changed, with blocks presented in multiple sizes rather than a single size.

Block Families for New-Look Sampler Quilts

One of the initial blocks, Spring Picnic, was a very simple star with a new, layered look. It got me started exploring the basic star outline, looking for new ways to break the star into patches. This led to the "Simple Stars" family of blocks on pages 48–52. I continued playing with other types of blocks, resulting in ten block families created for the book. The whole idea of sampler quilts made from blocks in the same family, from blocks with the same silhouette, followed soon after.

I had planned all along to include quilt suggestions on the block pages, but now I decided to add my new sampler quilt patterns. This section grew to include a couple of "medleys" made from four or five block types in a medallion, as well.

Bonus: Yardage and Quilt Planning Charts

The blocks in families, the quilt suggestions, and the new sampler quilts and medleys became the core of the book, though another focus emerged. The sampler quilts made the notion of substituting one block for another one an obvious way to make a single quilt suggestion serve as inspiration for a whole family of quilts. I realized that with so much inspiration, many of my readers were going to want help in planning their own quilts. Having written *Judy Martin's Ultimate Rotary Cutting Reference* and coauthored *Taking the Math Out of Making Patchwork Quilts*, I knew how helpful yardage charts and other quilt planning information can be to quiltmakers flying solo without a pattern. While yardage and quilt planning charts are not necessary to make the blocks and quilts in the book, and some quilters will be content with the patterns, I felt that the intermediate quilters would appreciate the charts. (The rest can line the birdcage with those pages if they like!)

Do It Your Way

As you can see, with one thing leading to another, the direction of the book changed substantially as work on it progressed. I hope that the result is a book that will lead you to experience the same kind of "aha!" moments of creative excitement that I felt. Nothing beats the thrill of expressing yourself creatively, of doing something *your* way.

Several Sizes and Colorings for Each Pattern

This book may go off in several directions, but it does so with a single-minded approach: do it *your* way. The choice of block and quilt sizes is just the start. Each block and sampler quilt is presented in at least three different color schemes to give you plenty of ideas for coloring your project however you want.

Ease into Making Your Own Designs

The quilt suggestions are just that; because they don't include yardage figures (and the charts at the back of the book do), you will feel more free to substitute another block from the same family and make the quilt your own. These quilts are accompanied by diagrams that help you see how the blocks are joined and the quilts assembled. They are also accompanied by charts that help you plan the quilt in any size you want.

Use Your Own Favorite Methods

Books of blocks have traditionally presented patterns with a minimum of words. Here, the quilt patterns, as well, are presented with a minimum of words and a wealth of illustrations. This means that even the methods are your own. No specific methods are detailed, so you are free to use your own favorite shortcuts and tools.

The Simplest of Patches

Because the patterns use only the three most basic shapes in quiltmaking, the square, the rectangle, and the most common triangle, any quiltmaker with a little experience already has the skills needed for any project in the book.

A Book to Grow with You

Whether you are introduced to this book in a class or find it on your own, I sincerely hope it leads you to the best quilts you have ever made and the best times you have ever had making them. Whatever your experience, this is a book that can grow with you on your quilting journey. Enjoy!

Important Pattern Information
Read this first!
At least read the subheads to make sure we are on the same wavelength.

All Patch Sizes are Cut Sizes

Patch sizes listed are the sizes you cut. They include seam allowances. To allow for ¼" seams, I have added ½" to the overall length and width measurements of squares and rectangles; ⅞" to the overall length and width of a square from which you will cut two triangles; and 1¼" to the overall length and width of a square from which you will cut four triangles. (The triangles need to have more added than squares because two—or four—triangles have more edges than a single square has.) If you will be using a method that requires different dimensions, subtract my seam allowances (above) and add the amount required for your own method.

Largest Patches are Listed First

In the block cutting charts, I list all patches for the blocks in each two-page spread. Some patches may not be needed for some blocks. The patches cut from the widest strips are listed first. If you cut these first, you can cut some of the smaller patches from fabric left over from cutting larger patches.

In a separate section of the cutting chart, I list patches that are needed for the quilts but not for the blocks. If you are making a quilt, be sure to cut these patches, which are sometimes large, in size order along with the block patches.

If Patch Dimensions are Not Listed

When a patch is a size that is not easily rotary cut, I may leave that size out on the cutting chart. If that is the case, choose another block size having patches that are more readily cut. Sometimes, I make a notation to use another patch. In that case, the two patches are the same size but have different grainlines. Wherever possible, I try to have straight grain around the block's edges.

If Measurements are Followed by "+"

The "+" means you should cut the patch halfway between the listed number and the next higher ⅛" marking on your ruler. (The patch measurement is in sixteenths of inches, which are probably not on your ruler.)

Patch Letters are Consistent

Throughout the book, a letter or number stands for the same patch. The size will change for a different block size, but patch size will be consistent from one block to another within a block size.

Exploded Piecing Diagrams Show Sequence

Each block and quilt in the book has a piecing diagram to illustrate the patches and other units it comprises. The upper left corner of the block or quilt diagram shows the parts fully exploded. To the right, more patches or units are joined to show the next step in the sequence. Below, more units, perhaps whole rows, are joined. The block patches to be sewn early are shown closer together than the patches that are sewn later.

Instructions are Minimal

The sampler quilt patterns include yardage figures, block quantities and colorings, and a quilt assembly diagram. For block cutting instructions and piecing diagrams, I refer you to the individual block patterns on pages 48–96. For a sampler, you will probably cut and sew block by block, anyway.

The quilts on the block pages do not include yardage. For each, you will find a quilt assembly diagram and a chart listing quilt sizes for various numbers and sizes of blocks. Use the charts at the back of the book to figure yardage requirements, or use scraps and don't worry about the yardage.

Some Quilts Have Units Besides the Blocks

Many of the quilts include the featured blocks as well as pieced borders, sashes, or other elements made from additional units. For the quilts on pages 48–95, these units are shown below the quilt or near the quilt piecing diagram (pages 96–112). Their patches are listed in the cutting chart for the blocks. When the sampler quilts and medleys on pages 6–47 have additional units, the units are shown beside the blocks. Cutting instructions for these patches are on the second page of the quilt pattern.

Border Measurements are Exact, Include Seams

For the quilts in this book, border measurements include ¼" seam allowances; they do not include any extra for insurance. If you feel more comfortable that way, cut them a little longer. I have allowed enough fabric to cut borders on the lengthwise grain.

If the Patches are Not Fitting Together

When patches appear to be too long or too short, the problem is nearly always your seam allowance. Take a little time to perfect your seams. Pin both ends and each joint of a seam if it helps you achieve the accuracy you desire. Finally, avoid stretching the bias when you press.

Reader Block and Quilt Photos Displayed

Please consider sending me a snapshot of the blocks or quilts you make from *Knockout Blocks and Sampler Quilts*. An online gallery will showcase such examples. Go to www.judymartin.com to view the blocks and quilts or to get more information about submitting your photos.

Double Stars Sampler

I chose bright colors for all three versions of Double Stars Sampler because the stars just seem to shimmer that way. The centers of the larger blocks echo the smaller blocks in this original design. I planned the Double Stars and Simple Stars block families specifically to work together in this fashion. Wandering Stars also complement the blocks shown here.

Block Selection

6" Blocks Used
pp. 48–52: Simple
   Stars Family
p. 57: Evening Star

12" Blocks Used
pp. 58–62 Double
   Stars Family

▲ Crib/Wall Quilt

Yardage
Crib/Wall Quilt

1¾ yds. Black

¾ yd. Purple

1⅜ yds. Various Brights

3¼ yds. Backing
  2 panels 27" x 53"

½ yd. Binding
  2" wide x 6 yds. long

53" x 53" Batting

Twin/Double Quilt ▶

Yardage
Twin/Double Quilt

2½ yds. Med. Pink

1½ yds. Bright Coral

2⅞ yds. Purple

1¾ yds. Yellow

3½ yds. Various Brights

9 yds. Backing
  3 panels 31" x 101"

¾ yd. Binding
  2" wide x 11 yds. long

89" x 101" Batting

Quilt Sizes

Crib/Wall Quilt
48" x 48"
6 large blocks
6 small blocks
set in 3 staggered
    rows

Twin/Dbl. Quilt
84" x 96"
28 large blocks
28 small blocks
set in 7 staggered
    rows

Queen Quilt
96" x 102"
35 large blocks
35 small blocks
set in 7 staggered
    rows

Cutting for Borders and Sets (all sizes)

☐ **#51:** cut 6½" squares for alternate blocks

☐ **#50:** cut 3½" squares for Unit 1 in borders

Yardage
Queen Quilt

2¾ yds. Turquoise

4⅞ yds. Blue

2⅛ yds. Yellow

4⅜ yds. Various Brights

9½ yds. Backing
    3 panels 35" x 107"

¾ yd. Binding
    2" wide x 12 yds. long

101" x 107" Batting

Queen Quilt ▼

Crib/Wall Blocks

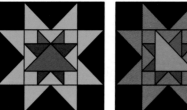

make 1
(12")
As You Like It
page 60

make 1
(12")
Opening Day
page 58

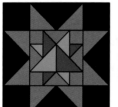

make 1
(12")
Pacific Star
page 62

make 1
(12")
Woodworker's
Puzzle, page 61

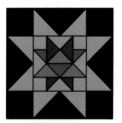

make 1
(12")
Cheerful Dawn
page 58

make 1
(12")
Rising Star
page 58

make 1
(6")
Wichita
Star, pg 52

make 1
(6")
North Star
page 50

make 1
(6")
Broadway
Star, pg 51

make 1
(6")
Movie Star
page 48

make 1
(6")
Evening
Star, pg 57

make 1
(6")
Moravian
Star, pg 52

Crib/Wall Quilt Assembly

Unit 1

Opening Day | #51 Movie Star | As You Like It | Eve Star | #51

Wichi Star | #51 | Rising Star | #51 | North Star | Pacific Star

Cheerful Dawn | #51 | Broad-way | Wood-worker's Puzzle | Mora-vian | #51

Unit 1

#51
cut
6

50
cut
56

50
cut
56

50 50
50 50
make 28
(6")
Unit 1

(cutting, page 7)

Note that some blocks may be turned differently from the way they appear on the block pages.

Twin/Double Blocks

make 2
(12")
Twilight Star
page 58

make 3
(12")
Celestial Light
page 60

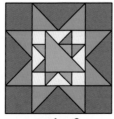

make 2
(12")
My Heart Leaps
Up, page 60

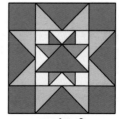

make 3
(12")
As You Like It
page 60

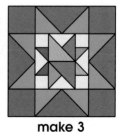

make 3
(12")
Shady Lanes
page 60

Twin/Double Blocks

make 3 (12")
Woodworker's Puzzle, page 61

make 2 (6")
Spring Picnic page 48

make 3 (6")
Movie Star page 48

make 2 (6")
Flag Day page 48

make 4 (6")
Evening Star page 57

make 4 (6")
Star of Heartland, page 51

make 4 (6")
Moravian Star, pg 52

make 4 (6")
Broadway Star, pg 51

make 3 (6")
Branson Beauty, pg 52

make 2 (6")
Wichita Star page 52

50
cut 112

50
cut 112

#51
cut 28

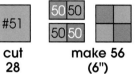

make 56 (6")
Unit 1

(cutting, page 7)

make 3 (12")
Pacific Star page 62

make 3 (12")
Rising Star page 58

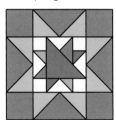

make 3 (12")
Opening Day page 58

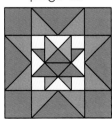

make 3 (12")
Cheerful Dawn page 58

Twin/Double Quilt Assembly

9

Queen Blocks

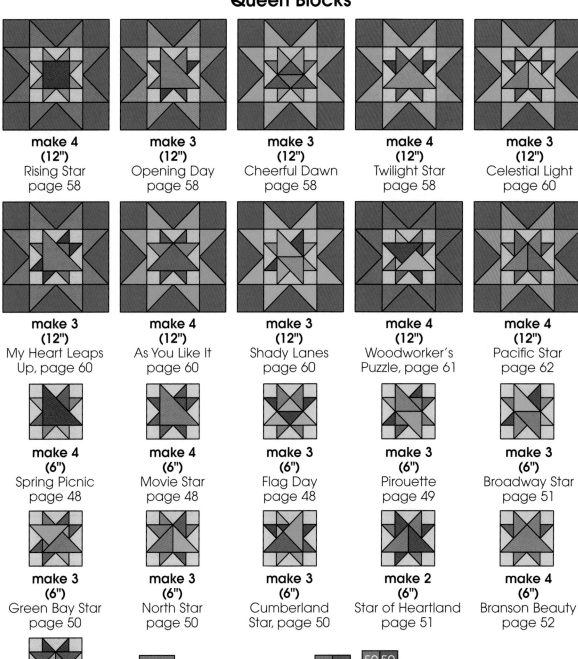

make 4
(12")
Rising Star
page 58

make 3
(12")
Opening Day
page 58

make 3
(12")
Cheerful Dawn
page 58

make 4
(12")
Twilight Star
page 58

make 3
(12")
Celestial Light
page 60

make 3
(12")
My Heart Leaps
Up, page 60

make 4
(12")
As You Like It
page 60

make 3
(12")
Shady Lanes
page 60

make 4
(12")
Woodworker's
Puzzle, page 61

make 4
(12")
Pacific Star
page 62

make 4
(6")
Spring Picnic
page 48

make 4
(6")
Movie Star
page 48

make 3
(6")
Flag Day
page 48

make 3
(6")
Pirouette
page 49

make 3
(6")
Broadway Star
page 51

make 3
(6")
Green Bay Star
page 50

make 3
(6")
North Star
page 50

make 3
(6")
Cumberland
Star, page 50

make 2
(6")
Star of Heartland
page 51

make 4
(6")
Branson Beauty
page 52

make 3
(6")
Moravian Star
page 52

cut
35

cut
124

cut
124

(cutting, page 7)

make 62
(6")
Unit 1

10

Queen Quilt Assembly

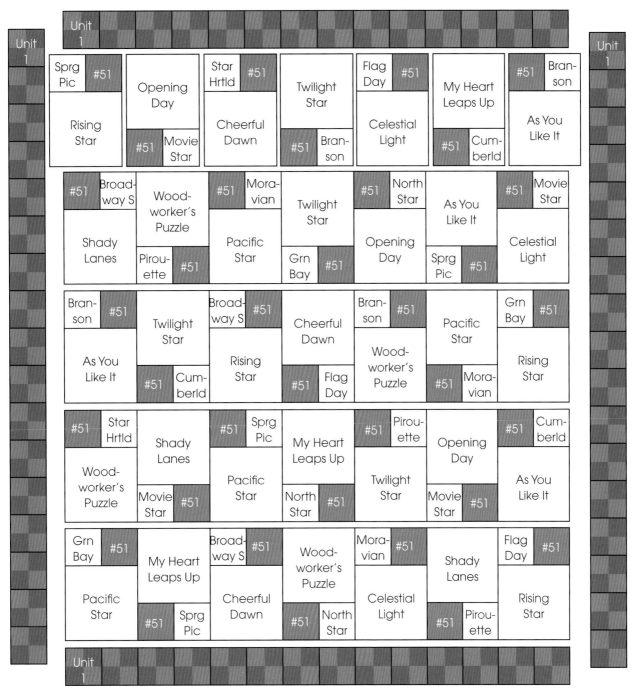

Virginia Stars Sampler

Sometimes, my previous designs are the inspiration for a new pattern. This quilt has the same set I devised for Shakespeare in the Park in my *Creative Pattern Book*. Here, I have substituted a variety of star blocks for the Rising Stars in that quilt.

Block Selection

12" Blocks Used
p. 53: Monticello
Electric Star
p. 54: Irish Star
Mississippi Star
p. 55: Mansfield Park
p. 56:
Remembrance

New England Star
Star of the Plains
p. 66: Virginia Star
Virginia Reel

6" Block Used
p. 57: Evening Star

▲ **Crib/Wall Quilt**

**Yardage
Crib/Wall Quilt**

2½ yds. Cream

3¼ yds. Red

3⅞ yds. Backing
 2 panels 33" x 65"

½ yd. Binding
 2" wide x 7 yds. long

65" x 65" Batting

Twin/Double Quilt ▶

**Yardage
Twin/Double Quilt**

5 yds. Cream

5¾ yds. Blues

8¾ yds. Backing
 3 panels 28" x 99"

¾ yd. Binding
 2" wide x 10 yds. long

82" x 99" Batting

Quilt Sizes

Crib/Wall Quilt
59½" x 59½"
13 blocks
24 edge blocks
set 3 x 3
   diagonally

Twin/Double Quilt
76½" x 93½"
32 blocks
36 edge blocks
set 4 x 5
   diagonally

Queen Quilt
99½" x 99½"
41 blocks
40 edge blocks
set 5 x 5
   diagonally

Yardage
Queen Quilt
6 yds. Pastels

8 yds. Brights

9¼ yds. Backing
   3 panels 36" x 105"

¾ yd. Binding
   2" wide x 12 yds. long

105" x 105" Batting

Cutting for Sets and Borders (all quilt sizes)
- ⊠ **#53:** cut 9¾" for edge triangles
- ◹ **#52:** cut 9⅜" for corner triangles
- ▢ **#51:** cut 6½" for plain squares

Queen Quilt ▼

13

Crib/Wall Blocks

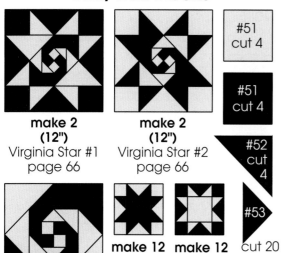

**make 2
(12")**
Virginia Star #1
page 66

**make 2
(12")**
Virginia Star #2
page 66

#51
cut 4

#51
cut 4

#52
cut 4

#53
cut 20

**make 9
(12")**
Virginia Reel
page 66

**make 12
(6")**
Eve Star
#1
page 57

**make 12
(6")**
Eve Star
#2
page 57

Crib/Wall Quilt Assembly

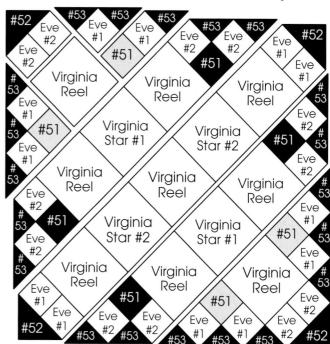

Twin/Double Cutting & Quilt Assembly

#51
cut 7

#51
cut 7

#53
cut 32

#52
cut 4

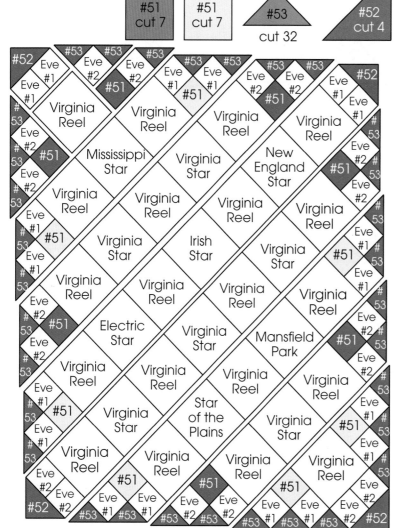

Twin/Double Blocks

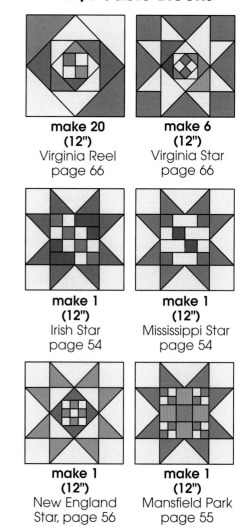

**make 20
(12")**
Virginia Reel
page 66

**make 6
(12")**
Virginia Star
page 66

**make 1
(12")**
Irish Star
page 54

**make 1
(12")**
Mississippi Star
page 54

**make 1
(12")**
New England
Star, page 56

**make 1
(12")**
Mansfield Park
page 55

Queen Blocks

**make 20
(6")**
Eve Star #1
page 57

**make 20
(6")**
Eve Star #2
page 57

#51
cut 8

#51
cut 8

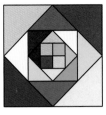

**make 25
(12")**
Virginia Reel
page 66

**make 1
(12")**
Monticello
page 53

**make 8
(12")**
Virginia Star
page 66

**make 1
(12")**
New England
Star, page 56

**make 1
(12")**
Irish Star
page 54

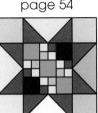

**make 1
(12")**
Remembrance
page 56

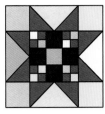

**make 1
(12")**
Mansfield Park
page 55

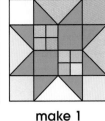

**make 1
(12")**
Electric Star
page 53

**make 1
(12")**
Mississippi Star
page 54

**make 1
(12")**
Star of Plains
page 56

#52
cut
4

#53
cut 36

Tw./Dbl. Blocks

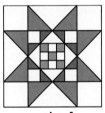

**make 1
(12")**
Star of Plains
page 56

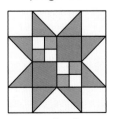

**make 1
(12")**
Electric Star
page 53

**make 18
(6")**
Eve Star
#1
page 57

**make 18
(6")**
Eve Star
#2
page 57

Queen Quilt Assembly

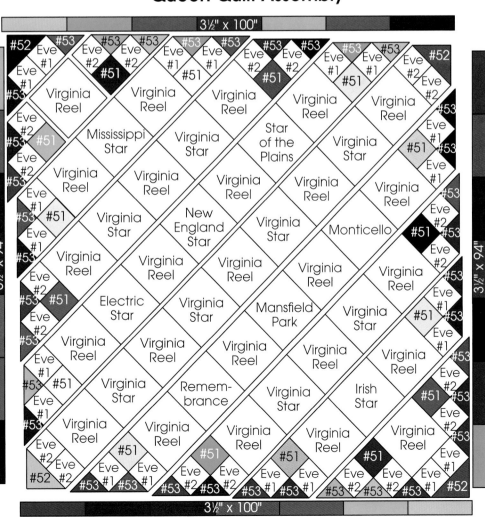

Exquisite Stars Sampler

The complex-looking stars in this quilt are from the Exquisite Stars and Shimmering Stars families. Each block has a large number of patches, but because the blocks are larger, you need fewer of them. The quilt is not especially more time-consuming than other ones that may be less impressive. The borders are a variation on my Staggered Star border.

Block Selection

15" Blocks Used
pp. 88–93: Shimmering Stars Family
pp. 94–95: Exquisite Stars Family

6" Blocks Used
p. 57: Evening Star

▲ Crib/Wall Quilt

Yardage
Crib/Wall Quilt
2 yds. Lt. Blue Bkgd.

1¾ yds. Various Brights

1⅝ yds. Blue Border

3½ yds. Backing
   2 panels 30" x 59"

½ yd. Binding
   2" wide x 7 yds. long

59" x 59" Batting

Twin/Double Quilt ▶

Yardage
Twin/Double Quilt
2⅝ yds. Light Blue

4 yds. Medium Blue

2¾ yds. Dark Blue

¾ yd. Dark Brown

¾ yd. Medium Brown

⅜ yd. Cream

9 yds. Backing
   3 panels 29" x 101"

¾ yd. Binding
   2" wide x 10 yds. long

83" x 101" Batting

Quilt Sizes

Crib/Wall Quilt
54" x 54"
5 lg., 12 sm. blks.
in a medallion

Twin/Double Quilt
78" x 96"
10 lg., 20 sm. blks.
set 2 x 3 w/sashes

Queen Quilt
96" x 96"
13 lg., 20 sm. blks.
set 3 x 3 w/sashes

Yardage
Queen Quilt
2 yds. Light Tan
  Background

4¼ yds. Dark Brown
  Background

4¼ yds. Various (Stars)

3 yds. Dk. Teal Border

1⅞ yd. Lt. Olive Border

9 yds. Backing
  3 panels 35" x 101"

¾ yd. Binding
  2" wide x 11 yds. long

101" x 101" Batting

Cutting for Borders and Sets

- ☐ **#65:** cut 15½" for borders (twin, queen)
- ☐ **#39:** cut 6½" x 15½" for borders (twin)
- ☐ **#42:** cut 6½" x 9½" for borders (twin, queen)
- ☐ **#51:** cut 6½" for borders (crib, twin, queen)
- ☒ **#54:** cut 4¼" for sashes (twin, queen)
- ☐ **#3:** cut 3½" x 14" for sashes (twin, queen)
- ☐ **#2:** cut 3½" x 12½" for sashes (twin, queen)
- ☐ **#38:** cut 3½" x 6½" for borders (crib, twin, queen)
- ☐ **#50:** cut 3½" for setting squares (twin, queen)
- ◺ **#55:** cut 2⅜" for sashes (twin, queen)

Queen Quilt ▼

Crib/Wall Blocks

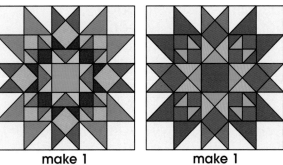

make 1
(15")
How Green Was My
Valley, page 94

make 1
(15")
Exquisite Star
page 94

make 1
(15")
Tea for Two
page 95

make 1
(15")
Ribbons & Bows
page 94

make 1
(15")
Liberty Belle
page 94

make 12
(6")
Evening
Star
page 57

#51
cut 12

#38
cut 12

Crib/Wall Quilt Assembly

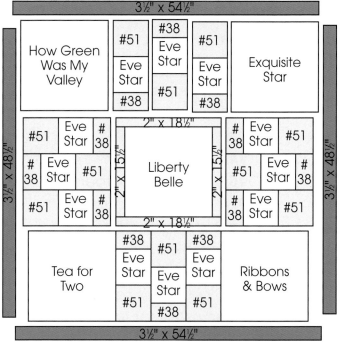

3½" x 54½"

How Green Was My Valley	#51	#38	#51	Exquisite Star
	Eve Star	Eve Star	Eve Star	
	#38	#51	#38	

3½" x 48½"

#51 | Eve Star | #38
#38 | Eve Star | #51
#51 | Eve Star | #38

2" x 18½"

Liberty Belle

2" x 15½"

#38 | Eve Star | #51
#51 | Eve Star | #38
#38 | Eve Star | #51

2" x 18½"

3½" x 48½"

Tea for Two	#38	#51	#38	Ribbons & Bows
	Eve Star		Eve Star	
	#51	Eve Star	#51	
		#38		

3½" x 54½"

Twin/Double Blocks

make 20
(6")
Evening Star
page 57

#55 #54
#55

make 8
Unit 1

make 1
(15")
How Green Was My
Valley, page 94

make 1
(15")
Tea for Two
page 95

Twin/Double Blocks

make 1
(15")
Peace in Our Time
page 90

make 1
(15")
Bayfield Star
page 88

make 1
(15")
Kansas Summer
page 90

make 1
(15")
Home Field
page 92

18

Twin/Double Blocks

**make 1
(15")**
Exquisite Star
page 94

**make 1
(15")**
Lakeside Cottage
page 91

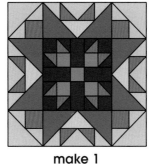

**make 1
(15")**
Over the River
page 88

**make 1
(15")**
Ribbons & Bows
page 94

Twin/Double Quilt Assembly

Twin/Dbl. Cutting

#55
cut 16

#54
cut 8

#50
cut 2

#38
cut 12

#51
cut 12

#42
cut 8

#39
cut 4

#3
cut 6

#2
cut 1

#65
cut 4

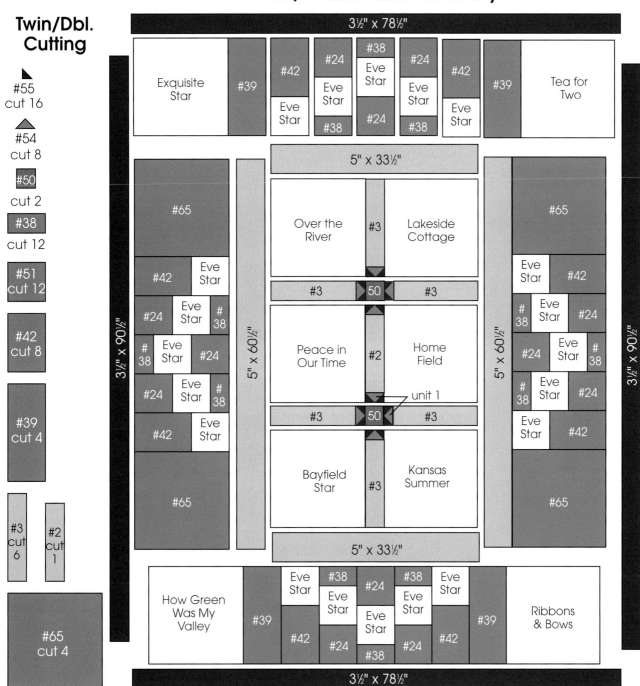

3½" x 78½"

Exquisite Star | #39 | #42 | Eve Star | #24 | #38 Eve Star | #24 | Eve Star | #42 | #39 | Tea for Two

Eve Star | #38 | #24 | #38 | Eve Star

5" x 33½"

#65

Over the River | #3 | Lakeside Cottage

#42 | Eve Star

#24 | Eve Star | #38

#38 | Eve Star | #24

#24 | Eve Star | #38

#42 | Eve Star

#65

5" x 60½"

#3 | 50 | #3

Peace in Our Time | #2 | Home Field

unit 1

#3 | 50 | #3

Bayfield Star | #3 | Kansas Summer

5" x 33½"

3½" x 90½"

#65

Eve Star | #42

#38 | Eve Star | #24

#24 | Eve Star | #38

#38 | Eve Star | #24

Eve Star | #42

#65

5" x 60½"

3½" x 90½"

How Green Was My Valley | #39 | Eve Star | #38 | #38 | Eve Star | #39 | Ribbons & Bows

Eve Star | #24 | Eve Star

#42 | #24 | #38 | #24 | #42

3½" x 78½"

19

Queen Blocks

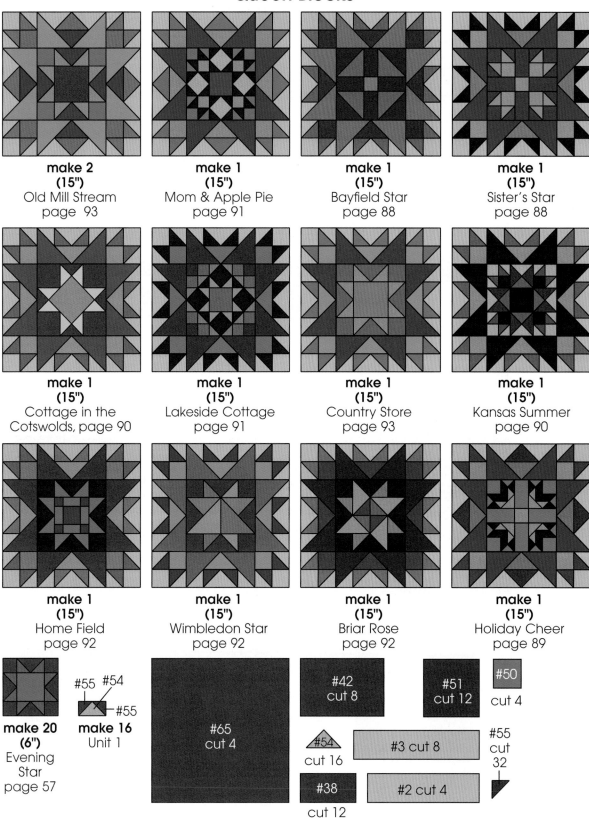

make 2
(15")
Old Mill Stream
page 93

make 1
(15")
Mom & Apple Pie
page 91

make 1
(15")
Bayfield Star
page 88

make 1
(15")
Sister's Star
page 88

make 1
(15")
Cottage in the
Cotswolds, page 90

make 1
(15")
Lakeside Cottage
page 91

make 1
(15")
Country Store
page 93

make 1
(15")
Kansas Summer
page 90

make 1
(15")
Home Field
page 92

make 1
(15")
Wimbledon Star
page 92

make 1
(15")
Briar Rose
page 92

make 1
(15")
Holiday Cheer
page 89

make 20
(6")
Evening
Star
page 57

#55 #54
#55

make 16
Unit 1

#65
cut 4

#42
cut 8

#54
cut 16

#3 cut 8

#51
cut 12

#50
cut 4

#55
cut
32

#38
cut 12

#2 cut 4

Queen Quilt Assembly

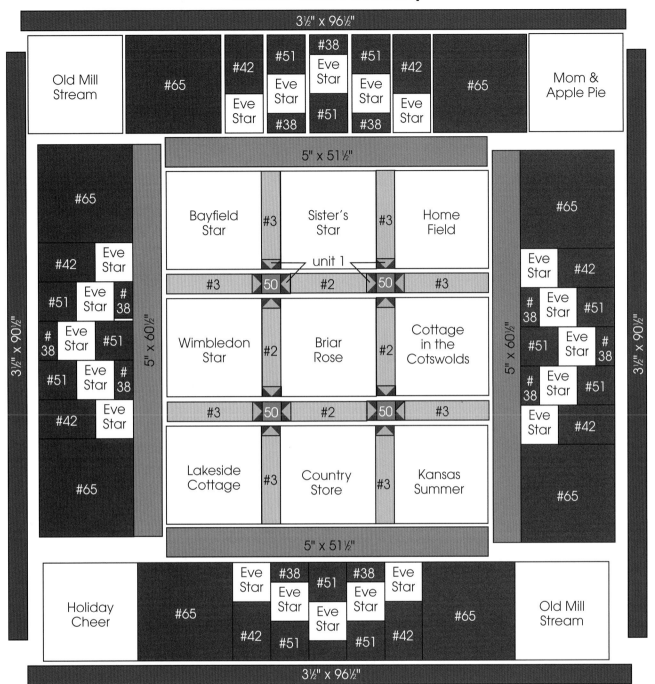

Varsity Medley

Varsity Medley is a winning quilt for the athletes and alumni in your life. Score high marks by making it in team colors that bring out the strong contrasts. This pattern would also make a delightful Christmas quilt in red and green. Varsity Medley uses blocks from the Stars & Chains and Free Spirit Families. I designed the blocks especially to form a border and corners in this diagonal set.

Block Selection

12" Blocks Used
p. 53: Monticello
p. 54: Irish Star
Mississippi Star
p. 73: Varsity Block

Sunshine State
p. 74: Three Sisters
Star in the Corner
Checkered Stripe
Checks in Corner

▲ Crib/Wall Quilt

Yardage
Crib/Wall Quilt

1½ yds. Cream

2¼ yds. Blue

1⅛ yd. Green

3½ yds. Backing
    2 panels 29" x 56"

½ yd. Binding
    2" wide x 6 yds. long

56" x 56" Batting

Twin/Double Quilt ▶

Yardage
Twin/Double Quilt

4¾ yds. Blues

4 yds. Browns

4½ yds. Cream

9½ yds. Backing
    3 panels 31" x 107"

¾ yd. Binding
    2" wide x 11 yds. long

90" x 107" Batting

Quilt Sizes

Crib/Wall Quilt
51" x 51"
13 blocks
set 3 x 3
    diagonally

Twin/Double Quilt
84⅞" x 101¾"
50 blocks
set 5 x 6
    diagonally

Queen Quilt
101¾" x 101¾"
57 blocks
set 6 x 6
    diagonally

**Yardage
Queen Quilt**

4⅝ yds. Cream

6 yds. Red

4⅝ yds. Green

9½ yds. Backing
    3 panels 37" x 107"

¾ yd. Binding
    2" wide x 12 yds. long

107" x 107" Batting

Cutting for Borders and Sets

⊠ **#57:** cut 18¼" for edge triangles (crib, twin, queen)

☐ **#56:** cut 12½" for alternate plain squares (queen)

◺ **#52:** cut 9⅜" for corner triangles (crib, twin, queen)

Queen Quilt ▼

Crib/Wall Blocks

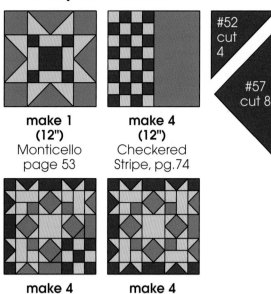

make 1
(12")
Monticello
page 53

make 4
(12")
Checkered
Stripe, pg.74

#52
cut
4

#57
cut 8

make 4
(12")
Sunshine State
page 73

make 4
(12")
Varsity Block
page 73

Crib/Wall Quilt Assembly

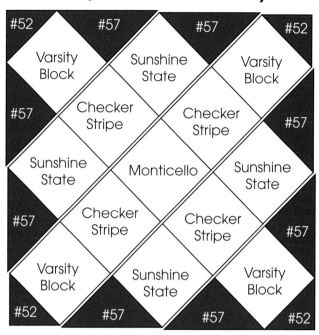

Twin/Double Quilt Assembly

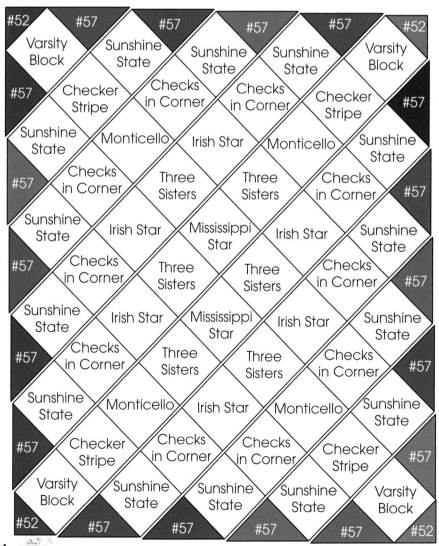

Twin/Double Blocks

make 2
(12")
Mississippi
Star, page 54

make 6
(12")
Three Sisters
page 74

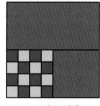

make 10
(12")
Checks in the
Corner, pg 74

make 4
(12")
Checkered
Stripe, pg 74

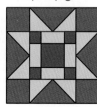

make 6
(12")
Irish Star
page 54

make 4
(12")
Monticello
page 53

Queen Blocks

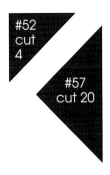

**make 1
(12")**
Monticello #1
page 53

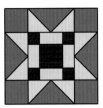

**make 4
(12")**
Monticello #2
page 53

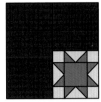

**make 4
(12")**
Star in the
Corner, pg 74

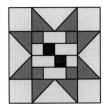

**make 4
(12")**
Mississippi Star
page 54

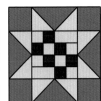

**make 8
(12")**
Irish Star
page 54

#56
cut 4

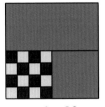

**make 12
(12")**
Checks in the
Corner, pg 74

**make 4
(12")**
Checkered
Stripe, pg 74

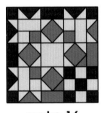

**make 16
(12")**
Sunshine State
page 73

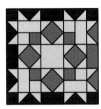

**make 4
(12")**
Varsity Block
page 73

Queen Quilt Assembly

Twin/Dbl. Blocks

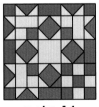

**make 14
(12")**
Sunshine
State, pg 73

**make 4
(12")**
Varsity Block
page 73

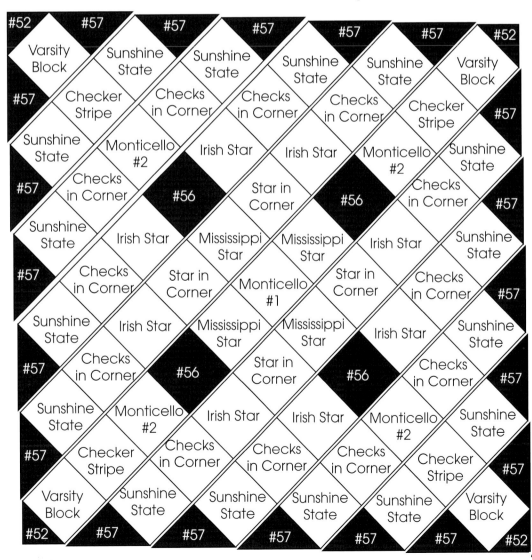

25

All in the Family Sampler

All in the Family would make a terrific presentation quilt on an anniversary or other family occasion. The Simple Stars and the larger Wandering Stars in this quilt have their differences as well as their similarities, just as members of a family do. The variety keeps things interesting. These blocks and quilts continue my exploration of superimposed motifs and mixed block sizes that I have used often in my designs.

Block Selection

12" Blocks Used
pp. 62–65: Wandering Stars Family

6" Blocks Used
pp. 48–52: Simple Stars Family
p. 57: Evening Star

▲ Crib/Wall Quilt

Yardage
Crib/Wall Quilt

1⅛ yds. Navy

1⅞ yds. Bright Blue

2 yds. Various Yellows

3½ yds. Backing
  2 panels 30" x 59"

½ yd. Binding
  2" wide x 7 yds. long

59" x 59" Batting

Twin/Double Quilt ▶

Yardage
Twin/Double Quilt

1⅝ yds. Lilac

3⅞ yds. Brights/Pastels

5¾ yds. Cream

9½ yds. Backing
  3 panels 29" x 107"

¾ yd. Binding
  2" wide x 11 yds. long

83" x 107" Batting

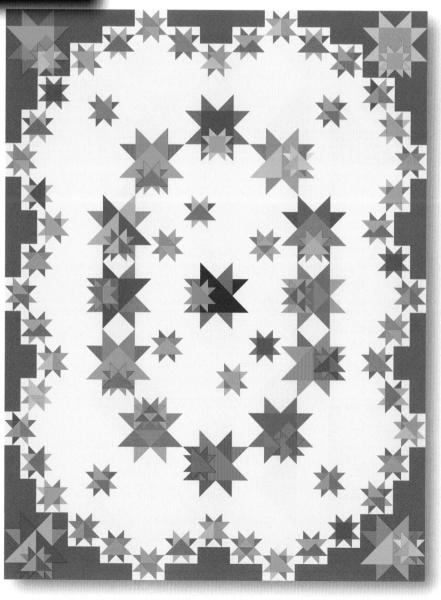

Quilt Sizes

Crib/Wall Quilt
54" x 54"
8 large blocks
25 small blocks
set staggered

Twin/Double Quilt
78" x 102"
17 large blocks
54 small blocks
set staggered

Queen Quilt
102" x 102"
21 large blocks
68 small blocks
set staggered

Cutting for Borders and Sets

#58: cut 6½" x 12½" for background (twin, queen)
#51: cut 6½" for bkgd., borders (crib, twin, queen)
#38: cut 3½" x 6½" for borders (crib, twin, queen)

Yardage
Queen Quilt

6¼ yds. Cream

4¾ yds. Pastels/Brights

3¼ yds. Butter Yellow

9½ yds. Backing
  3 panels 37" x 107"

¾ yd. Binding
  2" wide x 12 yds. long

107" x 107" Batting

Queen Quilt ▼

Crib/Wall Blocks

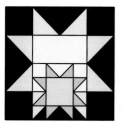

**make 1
(12")**
Me & My
Shadow page 63

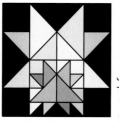

**make 1
(12")**
My Big Brother
page 64

**make 1
(12")**
Mother & Child
page 64

**make 1
(12")**
Double Puzzle
page 64

**make 1
(12")**
Autumn Wind
page 62

**make 1
(12")**
Like Father, Like
Son, page 64

**make 1
(12")**
Daddy's Princess
page 62

**make 1
(12")**
Spring in the Air
page 65

4 blocks with navy background for corners

Crib/Wall Quilt Assembly

navy

bright blue

**make 4
(6")**
Evening
Star, pg 57

**make 3
(6")**
Moravian
Star, pg 52

**make 3
(6")**
Flag Day
page 48

**make 3
(6")**
Broadway
Star, pg 51

#51
cut 8

#51
cut 8

#38
cut 8

#38
cut 8

**make 3
(6")**
Movie
Star, pg 48

**make 3
(6")**
Branson
page 52

**make 3
(6")**
Spring Pic-
nic, pg 48

**make 3
(6")**
North
Star, pg 50

Twin/Double Blocks

**make 1
(12")**
Mother & Child
page 64

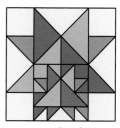

**make 1
(12")**
My Big Brother
page 64

Twin/Double Blocks

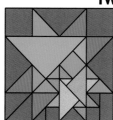

**make 1
(12")**
Double Puzzle
page 64

**make 1
(12")**
Me & My
Shadow, pg 63

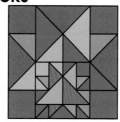

**make 1
(12")**
My Big Brother
page 64

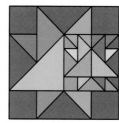

**make 1
(12")**
Mother & Child
page 64

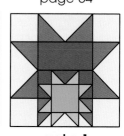

**make 1
(12")**
Me &My
Shadow, pg 63

Twin/Dbl. Blocks

make 5
(6")
Pirouette
page 49

make 3
(6")
North Star
page 50

make 4
(6")
Evening
Star, pg 57

make 3
(6")
Moravian
Star, pg 52

make 2
(6")
Heartland
page 51

make 2
(6")
Flag Day
page 48

make 2
(6")
Cumberld
page 50

make 5
(6")
Wichita St
page 52

make 3
(6")
Spring Pic-
nic, pg 48

make 6
(6")
Broadway
Star, pg 51

Twin/Double Quilt Assembly

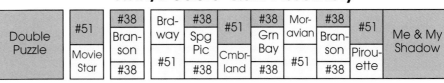

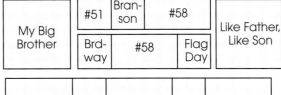

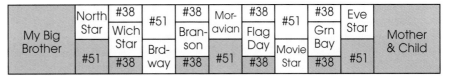

◄ **make 4**
(6")
Green Bay
Star, pg 50

◄ **make 7**
(6")
Movie Star
page 48

◄ **make 8**
(6")
Branson B
page 52

 #58 cut 16

 #51 cut 14

 #51 cut 12

 #38 cut 20

#38 cut 20

make 1
(12")
Double Puzzle
page 64

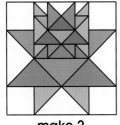

make 2
(12")
Autumn Wind
page 62

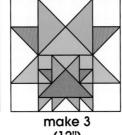

make 3
(12")
Like Father, Like
Son, page 64

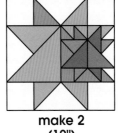

make 2
(12")
Daddy's Princess
page 62

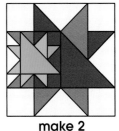

make 2
(12")
Spring in the Air
page 65

Queen Quilt Assembly

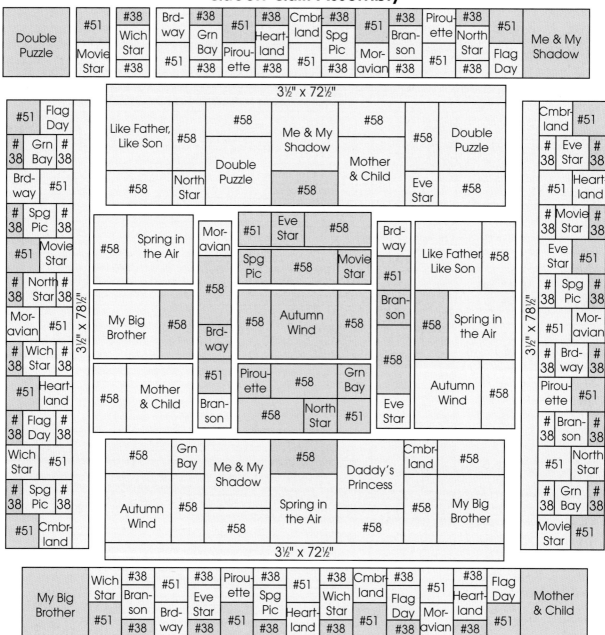

Queen Blocks

make 1
(12")
Autumn Wind
page 62

make 1
(12")
Double Puzzle
page 64

make 1
(12")
Me & My Shadow
page 63

make 1
(12")
My Big Brother
page 64

make 1
(12")
Mother & Child
page 64

make 1
(6")
Movie
Star, pg 48

make 1
(6")
Spring Pic-
nic, pg 48

make 1
(6")
Green Bay
Star, pg 50

make 1
(6")
Broadway
Star, pg 51

make 1
(6")
Pirouette
page 49

make 1
(6")
Evening
Star, pg 57

make 1
(6")
Branson
Beaut, p 52

make 1
(6")
North
Star, pg 50

make 2
(12")
Autumn Wind
page 62

make 2
(12")
Like Father, Like
Son, page 64

make 2
(12")
Me & My Shadow
page 63

make 2
(12")
Double Puzzle
page 64

make 1
(12")
Daddy's Princess
page 62

make 3
(12")
Spring in the Air
page 65

make 2
(12")
My Big Brother
page 64

make 2
(12")
Mother & Child
page 64

#58
cut 16

#58
cut 12

#38	#38
cut 24	cut 24
#51	#51
cut 12	cut 20

make 5
(6")
Broadway
Star, pg 51

make 5
(6")
Evening
Star, pg 57

make 5
(6")
Moravian
Star, pg 52

make 5
(6")
Heartland
Star, pg 51

make 5
(6")
Flag Day
page 48

make 5
(6")
Cumber-
land, pg 50

make 5
(6")
Wichita
Star, pg 52

make 5
(6")
Spring Pic-
nic, pg 48

make 4
(6")
Green Bay
Star, pg 50

make 4
(6")
Movie
Star, pg 48

make 4
(6")
Branson
Beaut, p 52

make 4
(6")
Pirouette
page 49

make 4
(6")
North Star
page 50

Summer Fields Sampler

I designed the Summer Fields family of blocks to complement the traditional Turkey Tracks. I changed the proportions for some block sizes to make the blocks compatible in size with most other blocks. This change in proportions also makes the blocks more graceful. The Celtic Chain block that you see in these quilts was inspired by the traditional Irish Chain, but its proportions, too, are changed. The combination of blocks makes an elegant quilt to show off your quilting.

Block Selection

12" Blocks Used pp. 82–87: Summer Fields Family

(Celtic Chains blks. alternate with a variety of blocks)

▲ **Crib/Wall Quilt**

Yardage
Crib/Wall Quilt

⅞ yd. Dk. Blue Violet

2½ yds. Lt. Blue Violet

1½ yds. Med. Blue Violet

3½ yds. Backing
   2 panels 30" x 58"

½ yd. Binding
   2" wide x 6 yds. long

58" x 58" Batting

Twin Quilt ▶

Yardage
Twin Quilt

1⅝ yds. Dark Blue

1½ yds. Aqua

5½ yds. Cream

⅜ yd. Coral Accent

6 yds. Backing
   2 panels 40" x 102"

¾ yd. Binding
   2" wide x 10 yds. long

78" x 102" Batting

Quilt Sizes

Crib/Wall Quilt
52½" x 52½"
9 blocks
set 3 x 3

Twin Quilt
72½" x 97"
15 blocks
set 3 x 5

Queen Quilt
102" x 102"
25 blocks
set 5 x 5

Cutting for Borders (all quilt sizes)

☒ **u:** cut 3" for borders

☐ **t:** cut 1¾" for borders

◩ **#1:** cut 1¾" for borders

Border Units (all sizes)

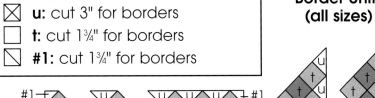

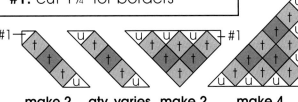

make 2
Unit 1

qty. varies
Unit 2
(pp. 34–35)

make 2
Unit 3

make 4
Unit 4

make 2
Unit 5

Yardage Queen Quilt

8¼ yds. Cream

1¾ yds. Dark Pink

2½ yds. Medium Pink

⅝ yds. Green

9½ yds. Backing
3 panels 37" x 107"

¾ yd. Binding
2" wide x 12 yds. long

107" x 107" Batting

Queen Quilt ▼

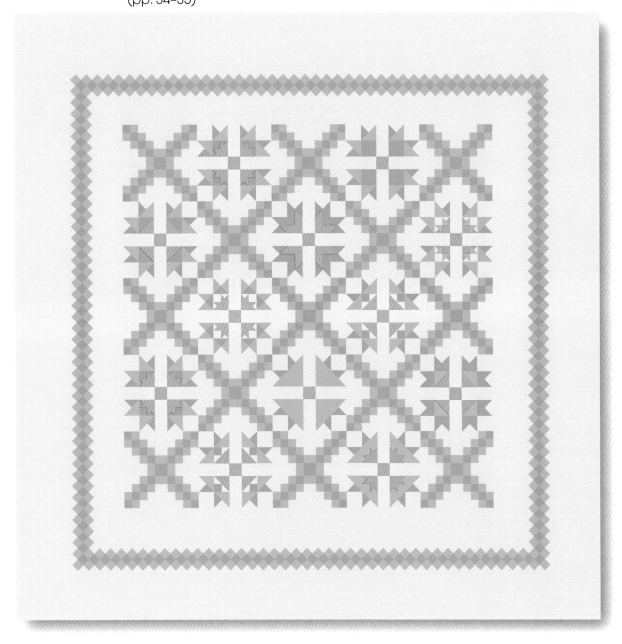

Crib/Wall Blocks

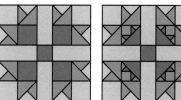

**make 1
(12")**
Guenevere
page 84

**make 1
(12")**
Jemima Puddle-
duck, page 82

**make 1
(12")**
Christmas
Goose, pg 86

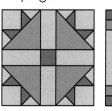

**make 1
(12")**
Turkey Tracks
page 84

**make 5
(12")**
Celtic Chain
page 83

Crib/Wall Units
page 33
2 Unit 1
90 Unit 2
2 Unit 3
4 Unit 4
2 Unit 5

Crib/Wall Quilt Assembly

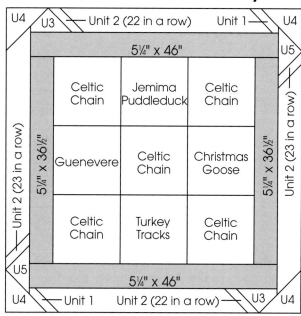
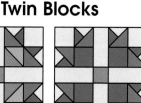

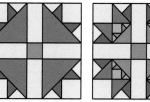

U4 — U3 — Unit 2 (22 in a row) — Unit 1 — U4

U5

5¼" x 46"

Celtic Chain	Jemima Puddleduck	Celtic Chain
Guenevere	Celtic Chain	Christmas Goose
Celtic Chain	Turkey Tracks	Celtic Chain

Unit 2 (23 in a row)   5¼" x 36½"   5¼" x 36½"   Unit 2 (23 in a row)

5¼" x 46"

U5

U4 — Unit 1 — Unit 2 (22 in a row) — U3 — U4

Twin Quilt Assembly

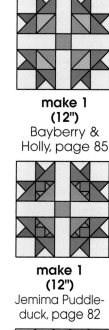
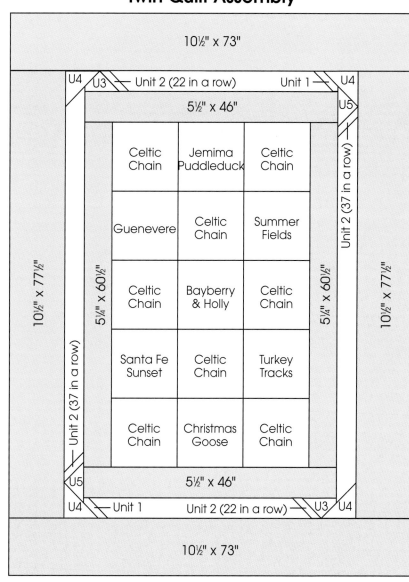

10½" x 73"

U4 U3 — Unit 2 (22 in a row) — Unit 1 — U4

U5

5½" x 46"

Celtic Chain	Jemima Puddleduck	Celtic Chain
Guenevere	Celtic Chain	Summer Fields
Celtic Chain	Bayberry & Holly	Celtic Chain
Santa Fe Sunset	Celtic Chain	Turkey Tracks
Celtic Chain	Christmas Goose	Celtic Chain

10½" x 77½"   5¼" x 60½"   5¼" x 60½"   10½" x 77½"

Unit 2 (37 in a row)   Unit 2 (37 in a row)

Unit 2 (37 in a row)

5½" x 46"

U5

U4 — Unit 1 — Unit 2 (22 in a row) — U3 U4

10½" x 73"

Twin Blocks

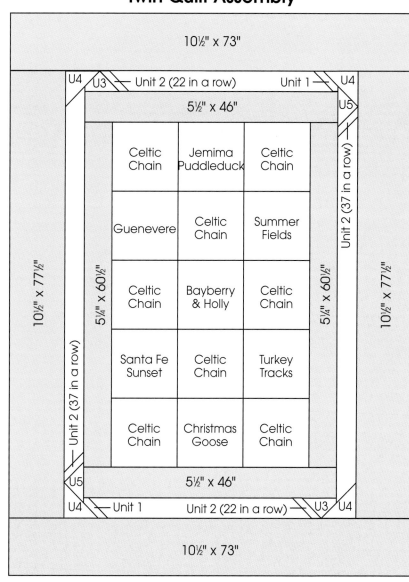

**make 1
(12")**
Bayberry &
Holly, page 85

**make 1
(12")**
Guenevere
page 84

**make 1
(12")**
Jemima Puddle-
duck, page 82

**make 1
(12")**
Christmas Goose
page 86

**make 1
(12")**
Turkey Tracks
page 84

**make 1
(12")**
Santa Fe
Sunset, pg 87

Queen Blocks

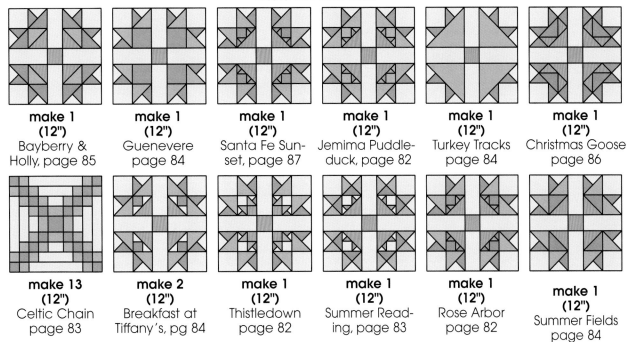

**make 1
(12")**
Bayberry &
Holly, page 85

**make 1
(12")**
Guenevere
page 84

**make 1
(12")**
Santa Fe Sun-
set, page 87

**make 1
(12")**
Jemima Puddle-
duck, page 82

**make 1
(12")**
Turkey Tracks
page 84

**make 1
(12")**
Christmas Goose
page 86

**make 13
(12")**
Celtic Chain
page 83

**make 2
(12")**
Breakfast at
Tiffany's, pg 84

**make 1
(12")**
Thistledown
page 82

**make 1
(12")**
Summer Read-
ing, page 83

**make 1
(12")**
Rose Arbor
page 82

**make 1
(12")**
Summer Fields
page 84

Queen Units
page 33
2 Unit 1
146 Unit 2
2 Unit 3
4 Unit 4
2 Unit 5

Twin Blocks

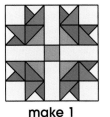

**make 1
(12")**
Summer Fields
page 84

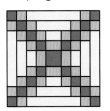

**make 8
(12")**
Celtic Chain
page 83

Twin Units
page 33
2 Unit 1
118 Unit 2
2 Unit 3
4 Unit 4
2 Unit 5

Queen Quilt Assembly

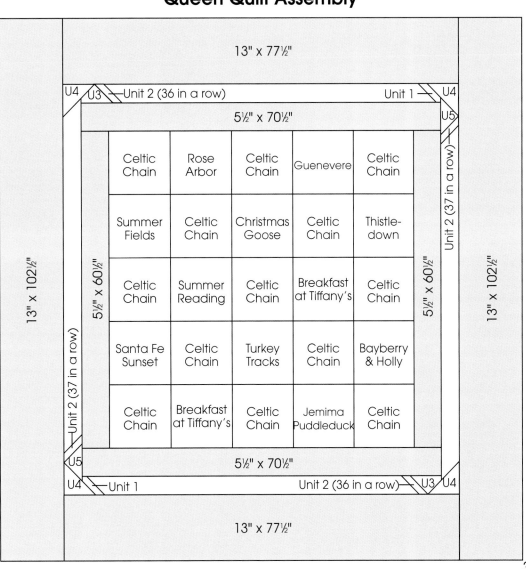

13" x 77½"

U4 U3 — Unit 2 (36 in a row)   Unit 1 — U4

5½" x 70½"   U5

Celtic Chain	Rose Arbor	Celtic Chain	Guenevere	Celtic Chain
Summer Fields	Celtic Chain	Christmas Goose	Celtic Chain	Thistle-down
Celtic Chain	Summer Reading	Celtic Chain	Breakfast at Tiffany's	Celtic Chain
Santa Fe Sunset	Celtic Chain	Turkey Tracks	Celtic Chain	Bayberry & Holly
Celtic Chain	Breakfast at Tiffany's	Celtic Chain	Jemima Puddleduck	Celtic Chain

13" x 102½"

5½" x 60½"

Unit 2 (37 in a row)

5½" x 60½"

Unit 2 (37 in a row)

13" x 102½"

U5

5½" x 70½"

U4 — Unit 1   Unit 2 (36 in a row) — U3 U4

13" x 77½"

Free Spirit Medley

Free Spirit is a medley of four repeating blocks from the Free Spirit family accented with simple Evening Star blocks. A Wind in the Willows center is embellished with borders of Dancing Pinwheels and Paul Revere's Ride to form a striking medallion. It would look great made from scraps or fat quarters with subtle color changes from block to block.

Block Selection

3" Blocks Used
p.76: Pinwheel

6" Blocks Used
p. 57: Evening Star
p.77: Dancing Pinwheels

12" Blocks Used
p. 71: Wind in the Willows
p. 72: Free Spirit
Paul Revere's Ride

▲ **Crib/Wall Quilt**

Yardage
Crib/Wall Quilt

1¼ yds. Blue

1¼ yds. Green

1 yd. Yellow

1½ yds. Cream

3⅛ yds. Backing
   2 panels 27" x 53"

½ yd. Binding
   2" wide x 6 yds. long

53" x 53" Batting

Twin Quilt ▶

Yardage
Twin Quilt

3¾ yds. Dark Blues

2½ yds. Medium Blues

4¼ yds. Ivory

6 yds. Backing
   2 panels 39" x 101"

¾ yd. Binding
   2" wide x 10 yds. long

77" x 101" Batting

Quilt Sizes

Crib/Wall Quilt
48" x 48"
13 large blocks
12 small blocks
  in a medallion

Twin Quilt
72" x 96"
26 large blocks
13 small blocks
64 mini Pinwheels
  in a medallion

Queen Quilt
96" x 96"
33 large blocks
56 small blocks
  in a medallion

Yardage
Queen Quilt

4½ yds. Blue

3¼ yds. Red

5½ yds. Off-White

9 yds. Backing
  3 panels 35" x 101"

¾ yd. Binding
  2" wide x 11 yds. long

101" x 101" Batting

Cutting for Unit 1 (twin, queen)

⊠ **#60:** cut 7¼" for star backgrounds

◻ **#59:** cut 3⅞" for star points

Queen Quilt ▼

Crib/Wall Quilt Assembly

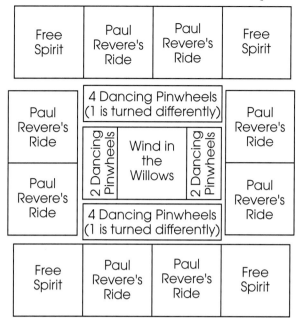

Free Spirit	Paul Revere's Ride	Paul Revere's Ride	Free Spirit
Paul Revere's Ride	4 Dancing Pinwheels (1 is turned differently)		Paul Revere's Ride
Paul Revere's Ride	2 Dancing Pinwheels	Wind in the Willows	2 Dancing Pinwheels	Paul Revere's Ride
	4 Dancing Pinwheels (1 is turned differently)		
Free Spirit	Paul Revere's Ride	Paul Revere's Ride	Free Spirit

Crib/Wall Blocks

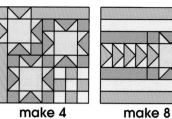

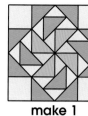

make 4 (12") Free Spirit page 72

make 8 (12") Paul Revere's Ride, page 72

make 1 (12") Wind in the Willows page 71

make 12 (6") Dancing Pinwheels page 77

Twin Blocks

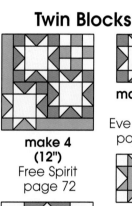

make 4 (12") Free Spirit page 72

make 10 (12") Wind in the Willows, pg. 71

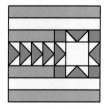

make 12 (12") Paul Revere's Ride, page 72

make 11 (6") Eve Star #1 page 57

make 2 (6") Eve Star #2 page 57

make 64 (3") Pinwheel page 76

make 14 Unit 1 (cutting, page 37)

59 ⟋ cut 28

#60 cut 14

Twin Quilt Assembly

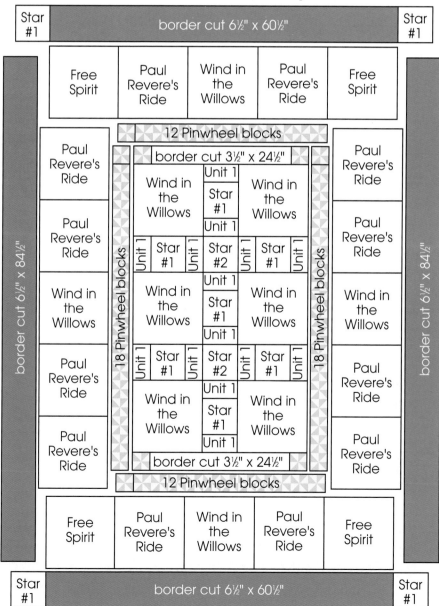

Queen Blocks

make 4
(12")
Free Spirit
page 72

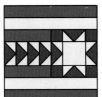
make 16
(12")
Paul Revere's Ride
page 72

make 13
(12")
Wind in the
Willows
page 71

make 36
(6")
Dancing Pin
page 77

make 16
(6")
Eve Star #1
page 57

make 4
(6")
Eve Star #2
page 57

make 24
Unit 1
(cutting,
page 37)

59 cut 48

#60
cut 24

E D E

Queen Quilt Assembly

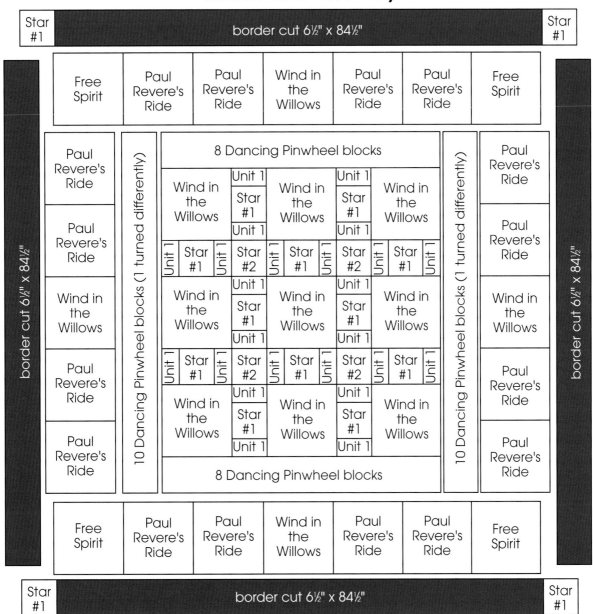

| Star #1 | border cut 6½" x 84½" | Star #1 |

39

Flying Stars Sampler

Twin and queen sizes are samplers of blocks from the Flying Stars family plus the Evening Star. In the crib/wall size, the quilt is a medallion featuring the Ivanhoe block and Evening Star corners. The sawtooth triangles make the blocks stand out.

Block Selection

10" Blocks Used
p. 57: Evening Star
pp. 67–70: Flying Stars Family

15" Block Used
p. 80: Ivanhoe

▲ Crib/Wall Quilt

Yardage
Crib/Wall Quilt

2 yds. Ivory Background

1⅝ yds. Pink

1 yd. Various Pastels

3½ yds. Backing
   2 panels 30" x 58"

½ yd. Binding
   2" wide x 6½ yds. long

58" x 58" Batting

Twin Quilt ▶

Yardage
Twin Quilt

5⅝ yds. Lt. Olive Background

2¾ yds. Olive Border

2⅝ yds. Various Darks

6⅛ yds. Backing
   2 panels 40" x 103"

¾ yd. Binding
   2" wide x 10 yds. long

78" x 103" Batting

Quilt Sizes

Crib/Wall Quilt
52½" x 52½"
5 blocks
set in a
  medallion

Twin Quilt
72½" x 97½"
6 blocks
set 2 x 3

Queen Quilt
107½" x 107½"
9 blocks
set 3 x 3

Cutting for Borders and Sets (all sizes)

☒ **#64:** cut 6¼" for units 2–5
◹ **#63:** cut 3⅜" for all units
☐ **#40:** cut 3" x 25½" for sashes
☐ **#41:** cut 3" x 20½" for Unit 4
☐ **#17:** cut 3" x 15½" for Unit 3/other
☐ **#62:** cut 3" for setting squares

Yardage
Queen Quilt

7¾ yds. Light Yellow Bkgd.

3¼ yds. Green Border

1⅝ yds. Teal Sashes

¼ yd. Rose Setting Squares

3¾ yds. Various Tones

10 yds. Backing
  3 panels 39" x 113"

¾ yd. Binding
  2" wide x 12½ yds. long

113" x 113" Batting

Queen Quilt ▼

Crib/Wall Blocks

#63 #64
make 48 **make 4**
Unit 1 Unit 2

#63
#64
#41
make 2 ▲
Unit 4

make 2 ▼
Unit 6

#64 #63

**make 1
(15")**
Ivanhoe
page 80

Twin Blocks

**make 1
(10")**
Fiery Star
page 67

**make 1
(10")**
Santa Bar-
bara pg 67

**make 1
(10")**
Chelsea
Morn, pg 68

**make 1
(10")**
Sea Breeze
page 68

**make 1
(10")**
Shooting
Star, pg 70

**make 1
(10")**
Evening
Star, pg 57

#63 #64
make 100 **make 16**
Unit 1 Unit 2

#17
F E E
make 12
Unit 3

#64 #63
#41
make 12
Unit 4

#62 #64 #64
make 12
Unit 5

**make
4
(10")**
Eve
Star
pg 57

63 62 64 63
cut cut cut cut
80 4 8 96

#17 cut 2

#41 cut 2

#63
cut
300

#62
cut
52

#17 cut 12

#41 cut 12

#40 cut 3

#63
cut
404

#64
cut
52

Crib/Wall Quilt Assembly

4¼" x 53"

62 | 6 Unit 1 | Unit 2 | 6 Unit 1 | 62

4¼" x 45½"

6 Unit 1
Unit 2
6 Unit 1

Evening
Star

8½" x 20½"
Unit 4

8½" x 20½"

Unit 6

#17 Ivanhoe #17

Unit 6

8½" x 20½"

Evening
Star

6 Unit 1
Unit 2
6 Unit 1

Evening
Star

Unit 4
8½" x 20½"

Evening
Star

4¼" x 45½"

6 Unit 1
Unit 2
6 Unit 1

62 | 6 Unit 1 | Unit 2 | 6 Unit 1 | 62

4¼" x 53"

Twin Quilt Assembly

4¼" x 73"

62 | 10 Unit 1 | Unit 2 | 10 Unit 1 | 62

3" x 53"

15 Unit 1
Unit 2
4¼" x 85½"

Unit 4
Unit 2
Unit 5 | Unit 3 | Fiery Star | Unit 3 | Unit 5
#40
Unit 5 | Unit 3 | Chelsea Morn | Unit 3 | Unit 5
Unit 2
Unit 4

Unit 4
Unit 2

15 Unit 1

4¼" x 90½"

3" x 53"

Unit 4
Unit 2
Unit 5 | Unit 3 | Sea Breeze | Unit 3 | Unit 5
#40
Unit 5 | Unit 3 | Shoot-ing Star | Unit 3 | Unit 5
Unit 2
Unit 4

Unit 2

4¼" x 85½"

3" x 53"

Unit 4
Unit 2
Unit 5 | Unit 3 | Eve Star | Unit 3 | Unit 5
#40
Unit 5 | Unit 3 | Santa Bar-bara | Unit 3 | Unit 5
Unit 2
Unit 4

Unit 4
Unit 2

15 Unit 1

4¼" x 90½"

3" x 53"

62 | 10 Unit 1 | Unit 2 | 10 Unit 1 | 62

4¼" x 73"

42

Queen Blocks

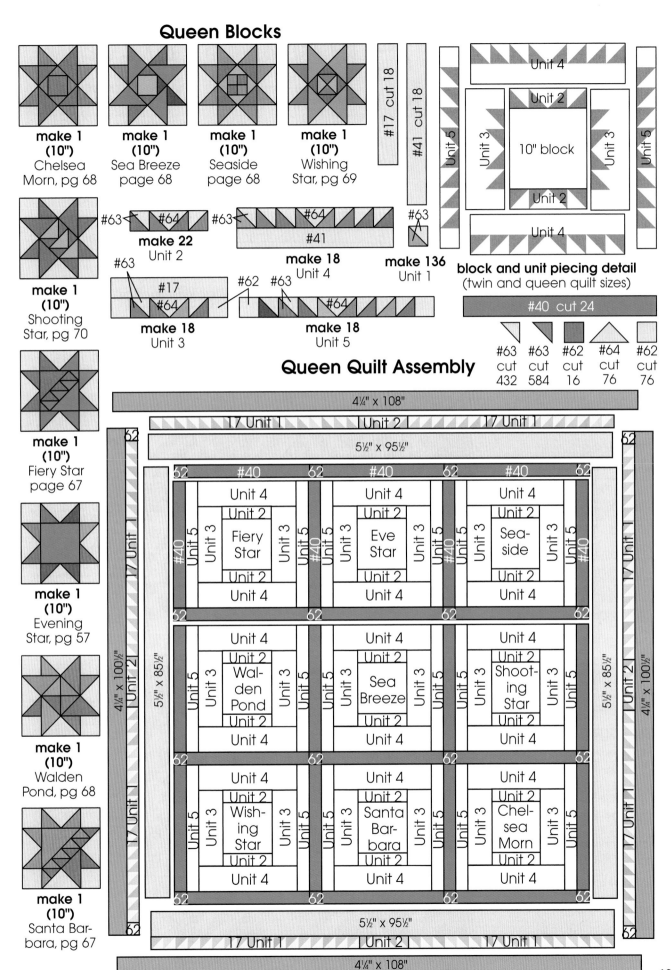

Stars & Stripes Forever

I designed Stars & Stripes Forever as a special Quilt of the Moment in the month following September 11, 2001. I got so many requests for the pattern after its run on the website that I decided to run it again in this book. This quilt is what I call a medley. It is made from several different blocks, but it is not technically a sampler quilt because the blocks repeat.

Block Selection

12" Blocks Used
p. 57 Gulf Coast
p. 58: Rising Star

6" Blocks Used
p. 57: Evening Star
p. 76: Rail Fence Checkerboard

▲ Crib/Wall Quilt

Yardage
Crib/Wall Quilt

1⅜ yds. Various Pastels

1½ yds. Off-White

1⅜ yds. Yellow

3⅜ yds. Backing
   2 panels 29" x 56"

½ yd. Binding
   2" wide x 6 yds. long

56" x 56" Batting

Twin Quilt ▶

Yardage
Twin Quilt

3½ yds. Red

3½ yds. White

2¾ yds. Blue

5⅝ yds. Backing
   2 panels 40" x 95"

¾ yd. Binding
   2" wide x 10 yds. long

78" x 95" Batting

Quilt Sizes

Crib/Wall Quilt
51" x 51"
1 large block
44 small blocks
set diagonally

Twin Quilt
73" x 90"
8 large blocks
86 small blocks
set diagonally

Queen Quilt
97" x 97"
13 large blocks
104 small blocks
set diagonally

Yardage
Queen Quilt
4¾ yds. Various Blues

3¼ yds. Various Greens

4½ yds. Tan Background

9 yds. Backing
   3 panels 35" x 102"

¾ yd. Binding
   2" wide x 11½ yds. long

102" x 102" Batting

Cutting for Borders and Sets (all quilt sizes)

⊠ **#53:** cut 9¾" for edge triangles (center & border)

◳ **#52:** cut 9⅜" for corners of quilt center

◺ **#66:** cut 5⅛" for border corners

Queen Quilt ▼

Crib/Wall Blocks

**make 1
(12")**
Rising Star
page 58

**make 16
(6")**
Evening Star
page 57

**make 20
(6")**
Rail Fence
page 76

**make 8
(6")**
Checkerboard
page 76

#53
cut 36

#66
cut 8

#52
cut 4

Crib/Wall Quilt Assembly

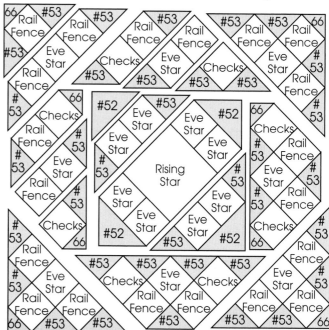

Twin Quilt Assembly

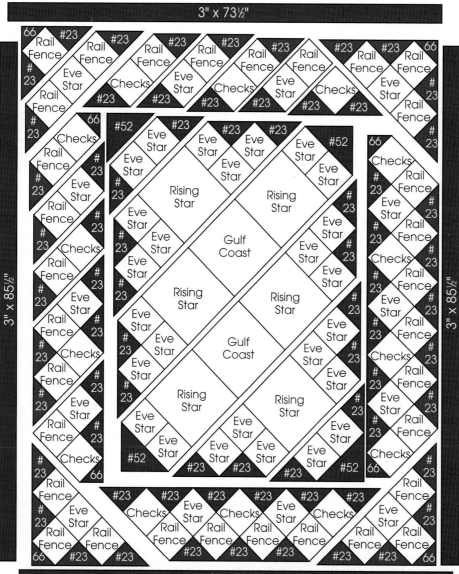

3" x 73½"

3" x 85½"

3" x 85½"

3" x 73½"

Twin Blocks

**make 6
(12")**
Rising Star
page 58

**make 2
(12")**
Gulf Coast
page 57

**make 40
(6")**
Evening
Star, pg 57

**make 14
(6")**
Checkerboard
page 76

**make 32
(6")**
Rail Fence
page 76

Twin Cutting

#53 cut 36

#52 cut 4

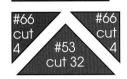

#66 cut 4

#66 cut 4

#53 cut 32

Queen Blocks

make 5 (12")
Rising Star
page 58

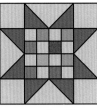

make 8 (12")
Gulf Coast
page 57

make 48 (6")
Evening Star, pg 57

make 20 (6")
Checkerboard
page 76

make 36 (6")
Rail Fence
page 76

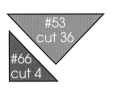

#53 cut 36

#66 cut 4

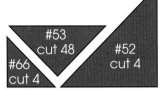

#53 cut 48

#66 cut 4

#52 cut 4

Queen Quilt Assembly

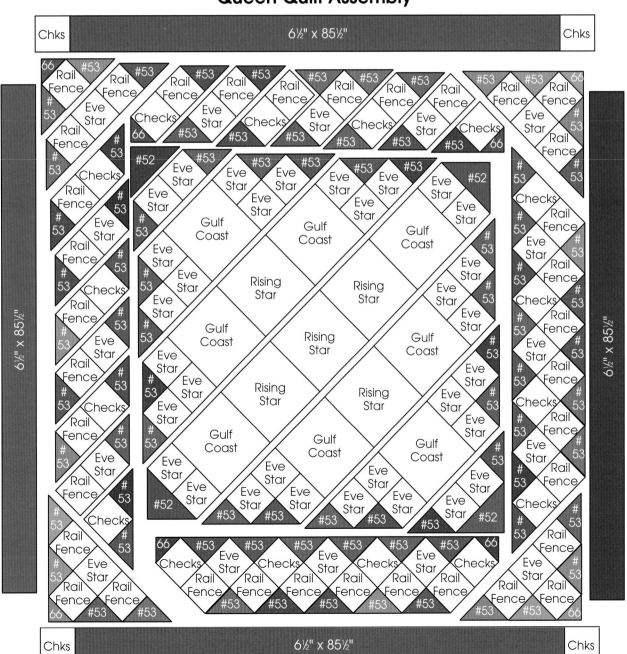

Spring Picnic

I designed this cheery star in April, 2001 as a Block of the Moment for my web site. I love the way it looks layered when you color the star points in matched pairs. It is one of the easiest star blocks you'll ever want to make.

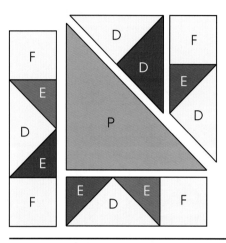

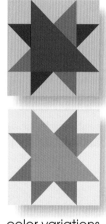

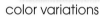

color variations

Spring Picnic

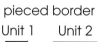

Quilt piecing diagram and size chart are on page 96.

pieced border

Unit 1   Unit 2

F   F

d

Movie Star

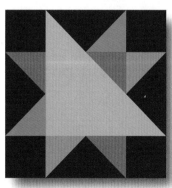

Movie Star is similar to Spring Picnic. However, in this block, the layering appears to be in a different sequence. This new star has fewer pieces than the standard eight-pointed star, and the shapes are every bit as simple.

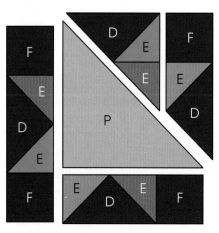

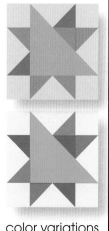

color variations

Flag Day

Flag Day is another block that resulted from my exploration of triangles that appear to be layered or interwoven to form stars. Coloring the block with different matched sets of triangles will result in a variety of looks.

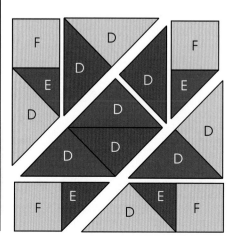

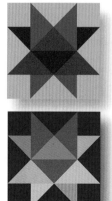

color variations

Pirouette

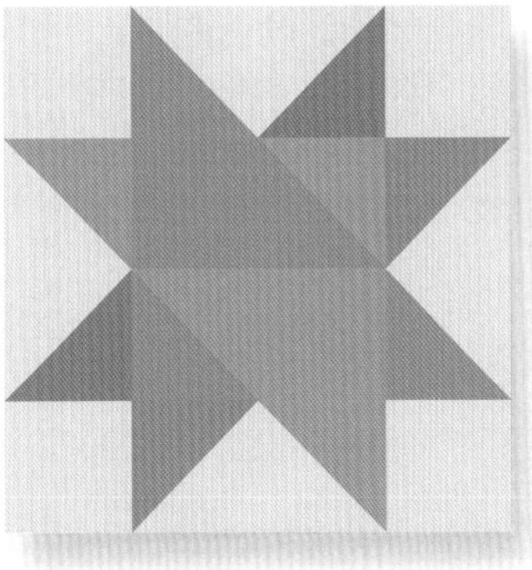

In Pirouette, which I designed for this book, one large triangle appears to pierce another. The dimensionality of this block makes Pirouette looks complex, but the cutting and sewing is, in fact, quite simple.

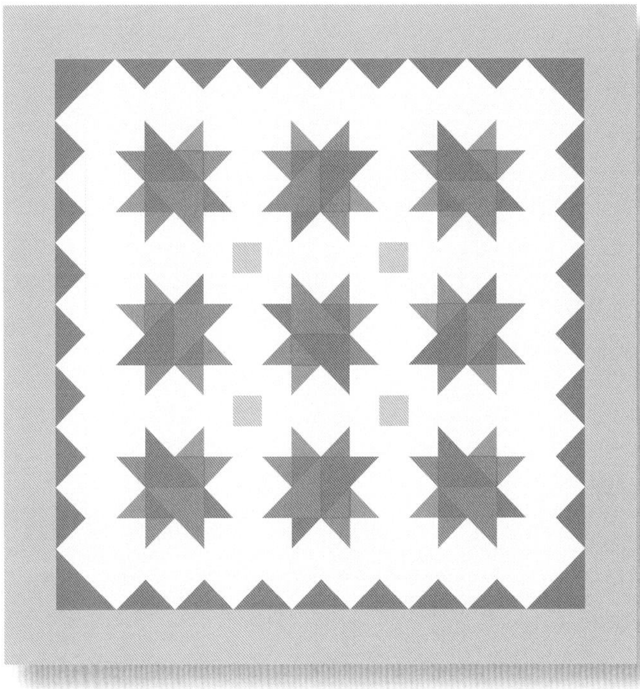

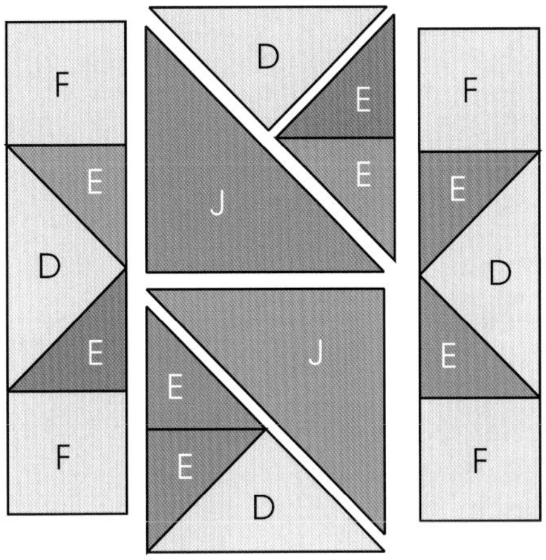

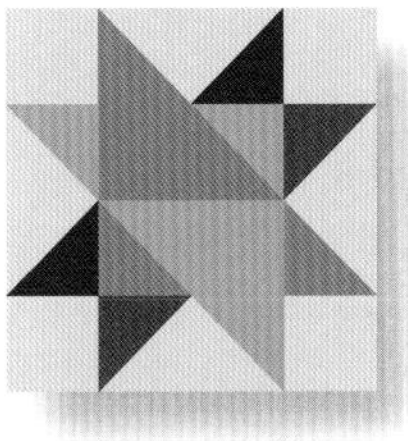

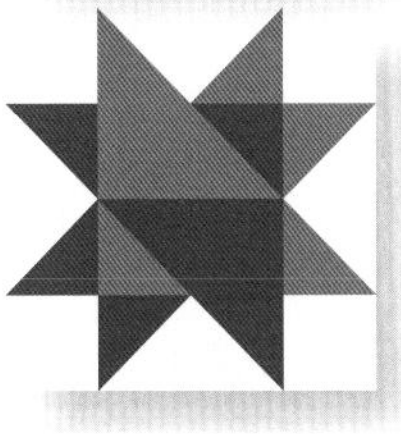

color variations

Pirouette

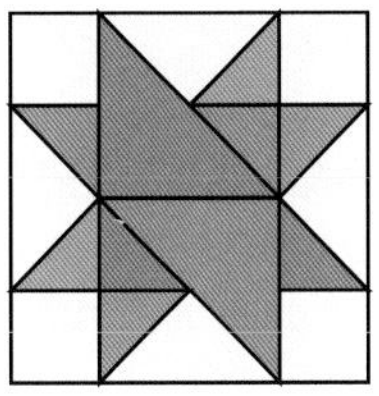

Quilt piecing diagram and size chart are on page 96.

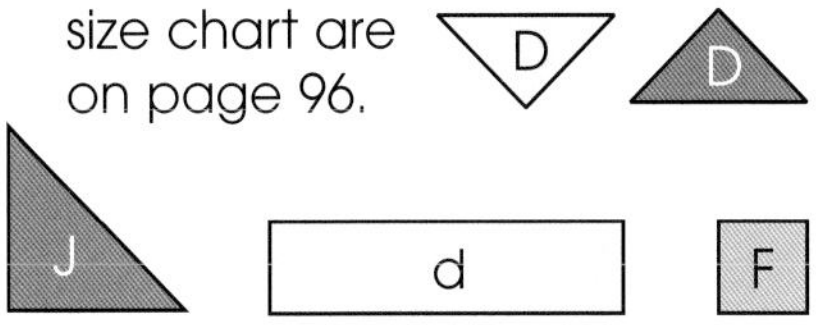

Patch Cutting for 5"–12" blocks on these two pages

Blk. Size:	5"	6"	7"	8"	9"	10"	12"
Block Patch	**Cutting Dimensions for Patches**						
P ⧅	4⅝"	5⅜"	6⅛"	6⅞"	7⅝"	8⅜"	9⅞"
D ⊠	3¾"	4¼"	4¾"	5¼"	5¾"	6¼"	7¼"
J ⧅	3⅜"	3⅞"	4⅜"	4⅞"	5⅜"	5⅞"	6⅞"
E ⧅	2⅛"	2⅜"	2⅝"	2⅞"	3⅛"	3⅜"	3⅞"
F □	1¾"	2"	2¼"	2½"	2¾"	3"	3½"
Quilt Patch d ▭	1¾" x 5½"	2" x 6½"	2¼" x 7½"	2½" x 8½"	2¾" x 9½"	3" x 10½"	3½" x 12½"

Notes

Green Bay Star

This new block looks dimensional with its triangles suggesting an assemblage of slotted parts. The effect can be heightened with shaded tones. The piecing diagram reveals that this is not as tricky as it appears.

Quilt diagram and size chart are on page 97.

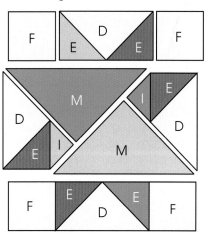

color variations

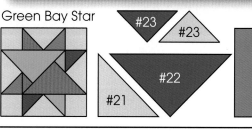

Green Bay Star

North Star

I designed this block to look dimensional. The pink, purple and turquoise version at left looks like arrowheads piercing one another. This block mixes well with the stars on pages 48–52 and on pages 58–65.

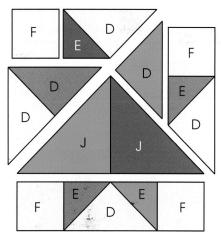

color variations

Cumberland Star

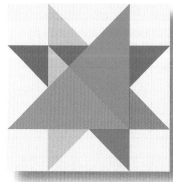

I once told my husband and kids that in my next life I want to be a box designer or fold-out book designer. For now, I'll design quilt blocks like this one. It looks like a cardboard assemblage, but I can put it in a soft, cozy quilt.

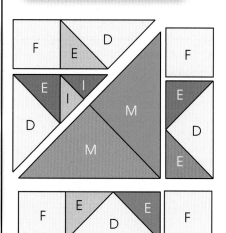

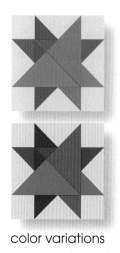

color variations

Star of the Heartland

This star is similar to my North Star, but I gave it a stronger vertical alignment. It works well in three colors, multi-colors, or in a carefully shaded monochromatic scheme. Star of the Heartland pairs perfectly with Pacific Star on page 62.

Broadway Star

I wanted to make a sampler quilt using a collection of dimensional-looking blocks having the same silhouette. Broadway Star is one of the blocks I designed for this purpose. I like the neon brights against the black.

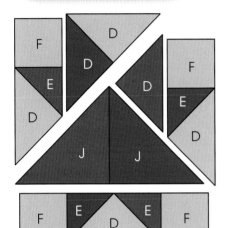

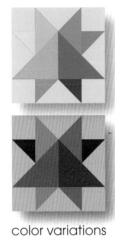

color variations

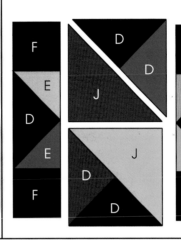

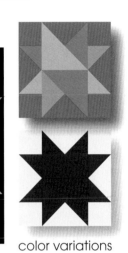

color variations

Patch Cutting for 5"–12" blocks on these two pages

Blk. Size:	5"	6"	7"	8"	9"	10"	12"
Block Patch	Cutting Dimensions for Patches						
M ⊠	5"	5¾"	6½"	7¼"	8"	8¾"	10¼"
D ⊠	3¾"	4¼"	4¾"	5¼"	5¾"	6¼"	7¼"
J ◻	3⅜"	3⅞"	4⅜"	4⅞"	5⅜"	5⅞"	6⅞"
I ⊠	2½"	2¾"	3"	3¼"	3½"	3¾"	4¼"
E ◻	2⅛"	2⅜"	2⅝"	2⅞"	3⅛"	3⅜"	3⅞"
F ☐	1¾"	2"	2¼"	2½"	2¾"	3"	3½"
Quilt Patch							
#22 ⊠	8¼+"	9¾"	11⅛"	12½"	14"	15⅜"	18¼"
#20 ☐	5½"	6½"	7½"	8½"	9½"	10½"	12½"
#23 ⊠	4¾"	5½"	6⅛+"	6⅞"	7⅝"	8¼+"	9¾"
#21 ◻	4⅜"	5⅛"	5¾+"	6½"	7¼"	7⅞+"	9⅜"

+ indicates a number halfway between the listed size and the next higher eighth inch.

Notes

Branson Beauty

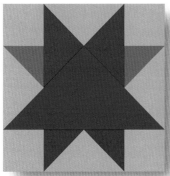

I love the simplicity of this new star. It is ideal for a smaller accent block or for use in a diminutive project. Substitute Branson Beauty for any of the simple stars in the quilts on pages 48–52.

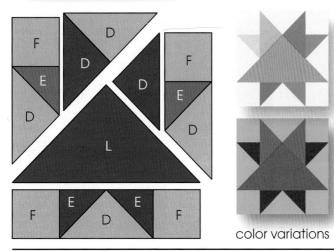

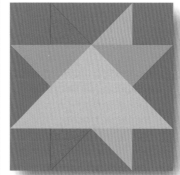

color variations

Wichita Star

Just a small change in patch placement turns Branson Beauty into my Wichita Star. It pairs well with a larger As You Like It block (page 60). You can add just a little asymmetry by turning the blocks differently.

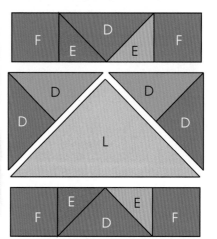

color variations

Moravian Star

This may be my favorite block. It reminds me of the folded Christmas stars from which I took its name. If you make the J triangles warmer and brighter than the D and E triangles, you will heighten the dimensionality.

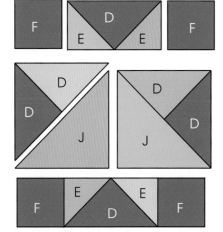

color variations

Moravian Star

Quilt piecing diagram and size chart are on page 97.

pieced sash

Monticello

Thomas Jefferson was a man of vision who expressed his inventive nature in his residence, Monticello. This block has roots in tradition, as does Jefferson's abode. I named the block to honor the statesman and his stately home.

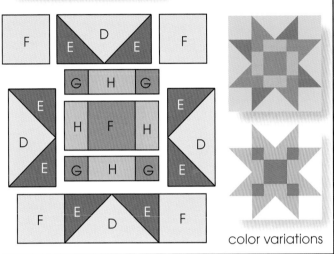

color variations

Electric Star

The squares that course through the center of this original block add a spark of excitement. The small squares are ideal for adding some high-voltage color. They can also add asymmetry to an otherwise static quilt. Watt fun!

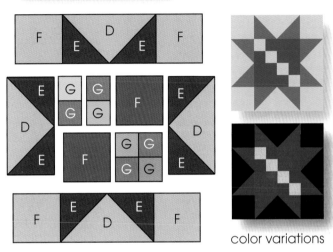

color variations

Patch Cutting for 6"–15" blocks on these two pages

Blk. Size:	6"	8"	9"	10"	12"	14"	15"
Block Patch	**Cutting Dimensions for Patches**						
L ⊠	7¼"	9¼"	10¼"	11¼"	13¼"	15¼"	16¼"
D ⊠	4¼"	5¼"	5¾"	6¼"	7¼"	8¼"	8¾"
J ◹	3⅞"	4⅞"	5⅜"	5⅞"	6⅞"	7⅞"	8⅜"
E ◹	2⅜"	2⅞"	3⅛"	3⅜"	3⅞"	4⅜"	4⅝"
F ☐	2"	2½"	2¾"	3"	3½"	4"	4¼"
H ▭	1¼" x 2"	1½" x 2½"	1⅝" x 2¾"	1¾" x 3"	2" x 3½"	2¼" x 4"	2⅜" x 4¼"
G ☐	1¼"	1½"	1⅝"	1¾"	2"	2¼"	2⅜"

Notes

Irish Star

This star results from my combining an Irish Chain with an Evening Star. In the quilt at right, I turned Irish Star blocks in every second row to suggest woven chains. Your choice of colors can accentuate either the stars or the chains.

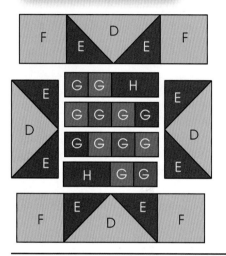

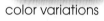

color variations

Irish Star   Dublin Chain

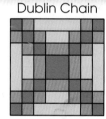

Quilt piecing diagram and size chart are on page 98.

border unit

Dublin Chain

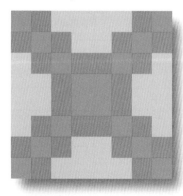

The Dublin Chain is my variation on an Irish Chain. The block center is enlarged to make it compatible with the blocks in the Stars & Chains family. I like this block best when the two colors of the chain blend rather than contrast sharply.

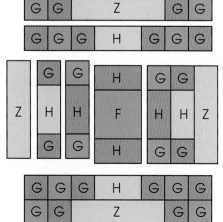

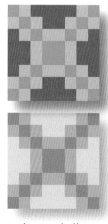

color variations

Mississippi Star

The Mississippi Star is a cousin to the Irish Star. Like the Irish Star, the Mississippi Star looks completely different depending on how you color the block. This and other blocks in the Stars & Chains family pair well with chain blocks and sets.

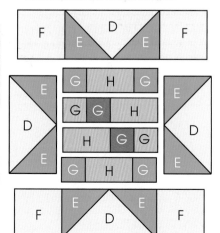

color variations

Mansfield Park

When I designed this block, the quilt came to me at once. If you like strip piecing, this is a good pattern for it. You can strip piece much of the block and quilt using the dimensions below for strips and subcuts rather than for patches.

Quilt piecing diagram and size chart are on page 98.

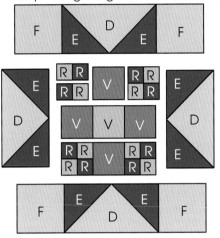

color variations

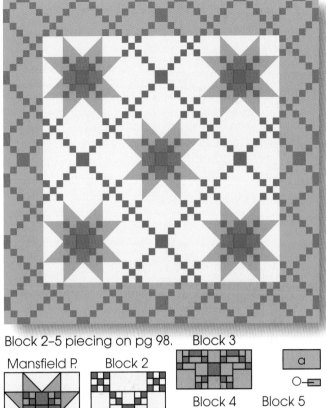

Block 2-5 piecing on pg 98.

Mansfield P.   Block 2 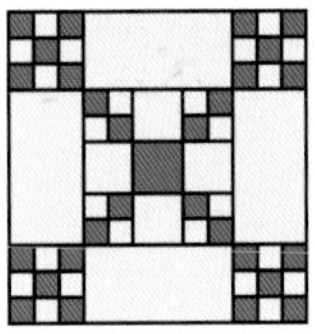   Block 3

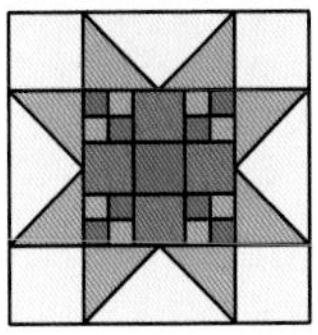

Block 4 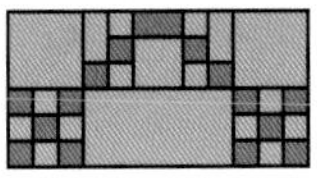   Block 5

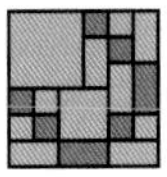

a

Patch Cutting for 6"-15" blocks on these two pages

Blk. Size:	6"	7½"	9"	12"	15"
Block Patch	Cutting Dimensions for Patches				
D ⊠	4¼"	5"	5¾"	7¼"	8¾"
E ◿	2⅜"	2¾"	3⅛"	3⅞"	4⅝"
F ☐	2"	2⅜"	2¾"	3½"	4¼"
V ☐	1½"	1¾"	2"	2½"	3"
Z ☐	1¼" x 3½"	1⅜+" x 4¼"	1⅝" x 5"	2" x 6½"	2⅜" x 8"
H ☐	1¼" x 2"	1⅜+" x 2⅜"	1⅝" x 2¾"	2" x 3½"	2⅜" x 4¼"
G ☐	1¼"	1⅜+"	1⅝"	2"	2⅜"
R ☐	1"	1⅛"	1¼"	1½"	1¾"
Quilt Patch					
a ☐	2" x 3½"	2⅜" x 4¼"	2¾" x 5"	3½" x 6½"	4¼" x 8"
O ☐	1" x 1½"	1⅛" x 1¾"	1¼" x 2"	1½" x 2½"	1¾" x 3"

+ indicates a number halfway between the listed size and the next higher eighth inch.

Notes

New England Star

The three stars on this page are limited in their range of sizes because the V and R patches are compatible with the other patches in just a few block sizes. This star mixes well with Nine-Patch blocks.

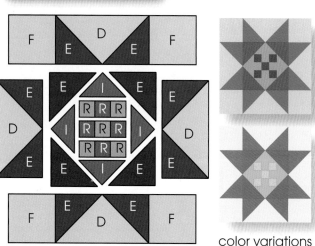

color variations

Star of the Plains

The Star of the Plains is a variation of my New England Star. If you can't decide which one you prefer, you can always mix the two blocks in a quilt. The slight change in rhythm will add interest to the quilt.

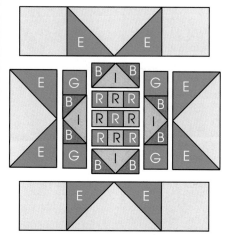

color variations

Remembrance

In this new block, a shaded chain marches across the star to create a strong diagonal element. The quilt arrangement echoes both the shading and the diagonals. Turning some blocks creates additional possibilities.

Quilt diagram and size chart are on page 99.

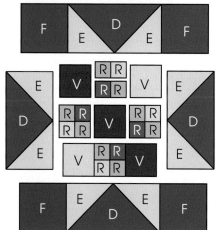

color variations

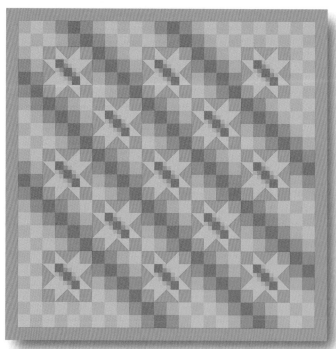

Remembrance   Checkerboard, pg 76

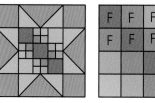

border units

Evening Star

This is perhaps the most popular of the traditional star blocks. Its simplicity, both in construction and in appearance, is a big part of the appeal. I often use this block in a small size in borders and other accents.

Gulf Coast

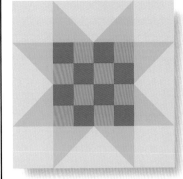

I haven't seen this block before, so I invented a name. Still, it is so basic that I won't take credit for designing it. The block works well with country stylings, and it pairs beautifully with a checkered border.

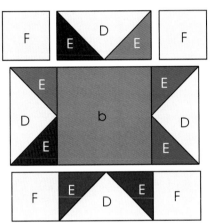

color variations

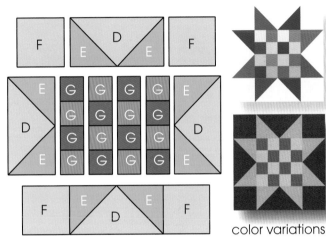

color variations

Patch Cutting for 5"–12" blocks on these two pages

Blk. Size:	5"	6"	7"	8"	9"	10"	12"
Block Patch	Cutting Dimensions for Patches						
D ⊠	3¾"	4¼"	4¾"	5¼"	5¾"	6¼"	7¼"
b ☐	3"	3½"	4"	4½"	5"	5½"	6½"
I ⊠	2½"	2¾"	3"	3¼"	3½"	3¾"	4¼"
E ◨	2⅛"	2⅜"	2⅝"	2⅞"	3⅛"	3⅜"	3⅞"
F ☐	1¾"	2"	2¼"	2½"	2¾"	3"	3½"
B ◨	1½"	1⅝"	1¾"	1⅞"	2"	2⅛"	2⅜"
V ☐		1½"			2"		2½"
G ☐	1⅛"	1¼"	1⅜"	1½"	1⅝"	1¾"	2"
R ☐		1"			1¼"		1½"

Notes

Rising Star

This is a traditional favorite and a favorite of mine, too. I particularly like it made from scrap fabrics. It is a perfect partner for the Evening Star block on page 57, which matches the center of the Rising Star.

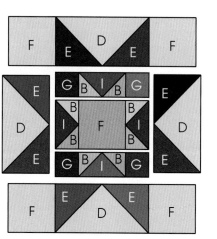

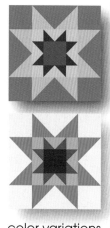

color variations

Opening Day

Opening Day is to Spring Picnic as Rising Star is to Evening Star. (Remember the analogy questions on those interminable exams?) I'd rather be watching a ballgame on Opening Day, when every player is a star and every team is undefeated.

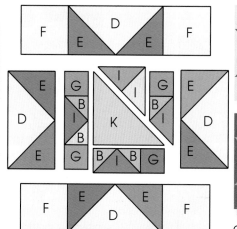

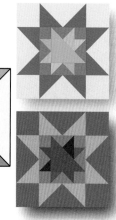

color variations

Cheerful Dawn

Stars in the morning sky? The name may be strange, but this new block is simply elegant. It is a partner block to Flag Day (p. 48). I like to combine these blocks, with Cheerful Dawn twice the size of Flag Day.

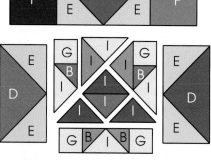

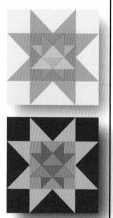

color variations

Twilight Star

Why not frame the day with beautiful star blocks? Couldn't you just imagine a quilt combining Twilight Star and Cheerful Dawn in the glorious colors of sunrise blending gradually into sunset? This block pairs with Branson Beauty, as well.

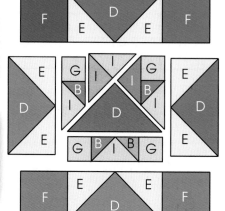

color variations

Rise Up So Early in the Morn

I combined a Rising Star with a Robbing Peter to Pay Paul coloring to make this block. It first appeared on my website in October of 2000. Different colorings result in surprisingly different looks.

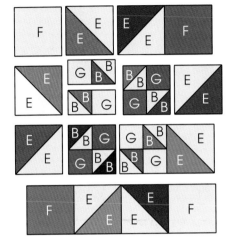

color variations

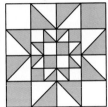

Rise Up So Early

Quilt piecing diagram and size chart are on page 99.

pieced sash

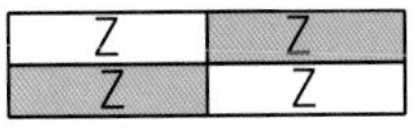

Z	Z
Z	Z

Unit 1

G	G
G	G

Patch Cutting for 6"–15" blocks on these two pages

Blk. Size:	6"	8"	9"	10"	12"	14"	15"
Block Patch	**Cutting Dimensions for Patches**						
D ⊠	4¼"	5¼"	5¾"	6¼"	7¼"	8¼"	8¾"
K �◲	3⅛"	3⅞"	4¼"	4⅝"	5⅜"	6⅛"	6½"
I ⊠	2¾"	3¼"	3½"	3¾"	4¼"	4¾"	5"
E ◲	2⅜"	2⅞"	3⅛"	3⅜"	3⅞"	4⅜"	4⅝"
F ☐	2"	2½"	2¾"	3"	3½"	4"	4¼"
B ◲	1⅝"	1⅞"	2"	2⅛"	2⅜"	2⅝"	2¾"
G ☐	1¼"	1½"	1⅝"	1¾"	2"	2¼"	2⅜"
Quilt Patch							
Z ☐	1¼" x 3½"	1½" x 4½"	1⅝" x 5"	1¾" x 5½"	2" x 6½"	2¼" x 7½"	2⅜" x 8"

Notes

Celestial Light

This original block has an airy delicacy. (The illusion of "holes" in the center star contribute to this, I suppose.) A light background for the small star makes the large star seem to have holes, as well. Use scrap fabrics to shade the patches for the illusion of depth.

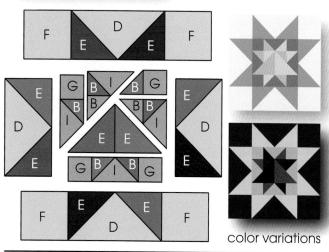

color variations

My Heart Leaps Up

Exuberant is how I would describe these colors. I suppose it was the colors that suggested the block's name. Make the quilt in rainbow colors if the namesake verse is a favorite of yours. This block is a partner to Movie Star (page 48).

color variations

As You Like It

I love a good Shakespeare play, and have borrowed several quilt and block names from the Bard. I always hope my readers will adapt my patterns as they like, so the name seemed appropriate. This block complements Wichita Star (page 52) perfectly.

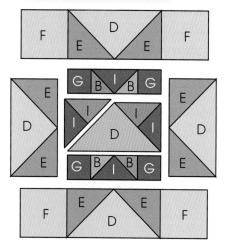
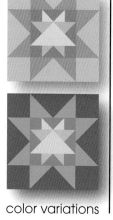

color variations

Shady Lanes

My first experience of trees that formed a canopy over entire neighborhoods made me a midwesterner at heart long before I abandoned the West Coast where I grew up. I am now content raising my children on a shady lane in Iowa.

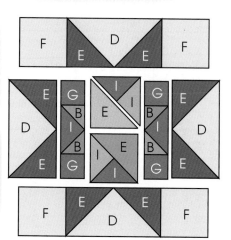

color variations

Woodworker's Puzzle

When I designed this block, it reminded me of a wooden puzzle box that my father once brought home from his travels. It would make a handsome quilt for a carpenter or cabinetmaker. I show it in a quilt with Green Bay Stars.

Quilt diagram and size chart are on page 100.

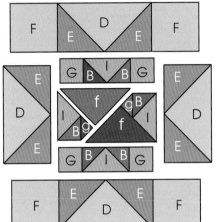

color variations

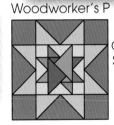

Woodworker's P

Green Bay Star can be made from Woodworkers's P center.

Green Bay Star, pg 50

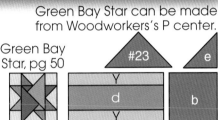

Patch Cutting for 6"–15" blocks on these two pages

Blk. Size:	6"	8"	9"	10"	12"	14"	15"
Block Patch	**Cutting Dimensions for Patches**						
D ⊠	4¼"	5¼"	5¾"	6¼"	7¼"	8¼"	8¾"
f ⊠	3½"	4¼"	4⅝"	5"	5¾"	6½"	6⅞"
K ◩	3⅛"	3⅞"	4¼"	4⅝"	5⅜"	6⅛"	6½"
I ⊠	2¾"	3¼"	3½"	3¾"	4¼"	4¾"	5"
E ◩	2⅜"	2⅞"	3⅛"	3⅜"	3⅞"	4⅜"	4⅝"
F ☐	2"	2½"	2¾"	3"	3½"	4"	4¼"
g ⊠	2"	2¼"	2⅜"	2½"	2¾"	3"	3⅛"
B ◩	1⅝"	1⅞"	2"	2⅛"	2⅜"	2⅝"	2¾"
G ☐	1¼"	1½"	1⅝"	1¾"	2"	2¼"	2⅜"
Quilt Patch							
#23 ⊠	5½"	6⅞"	7⅝"	8¼+"	9¾"	11⅛"	11¾+"
b ☐	3½"	4½"	5"	5½"	6½"	7½"	8"
e ◩	3"	3⅝+"	4+"	4⅜"	5⅛"	5¾+"	6⅛+"
d ☐	2" x 6½"	2½" x 8½"	2¾" x 9½"	3" x 10½"	3½" x 12½"	4" x 14½"	4¼" x 15½"
Y ☐	1¼" x 6½"	1½" x 8½"	1⅝" x 9½"	1¾" x 10½"	2 x 12½"	2¼" x 14½"	2⅜" x 15½"

+ indicates a number halfway between the listed size and the next higher eighth inch.

Pacific Star

Pacific Star combines a Rising Star with a Star of the Heartland. All of the Simple Stars and Double Stars blocks, as well as the Wandering Stars (below and on the following pages) have the same silhouette and work well in concert.

Quilt diagram and size chart are on page 100.

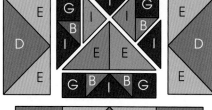

color variations

Pacific Star

Star of the Heartland can be made from center of Pacific Star.

Star of the Heartland, pg 51

b

Unit 1

Daddy's Princess

I call this family "Wandering Stars" because the smaller star seems to have wandered off from the block center. I like the dynamic asymmetry that results. I have explored this idea off and on for a few years, and it has yielded some of my favorite blocks.

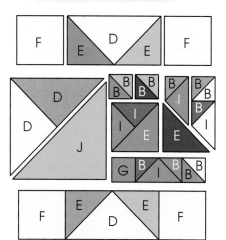

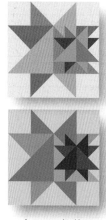

color variations

Autumn Wind

Fall is my favorite season (all the more beloved for my having been deprived of it for the first half of my life). The wind, the trees, the squirrels are all so busy that I feel energized, too. In lively fall colors, this new block conveys the thrill of the season.

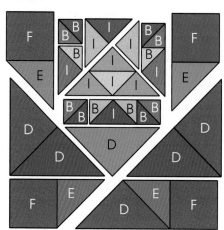

color variations

Me & My Shadow

This block makes me think of a small child fascinated with his big shadow. (I suppose it could also look like a Rising Star with a sagging midsection, or, if you turn it around, a Rising Star with a facelift.) It looks great accented with smaller stars.

Quilt piecing diagram and size chart are on page 101.

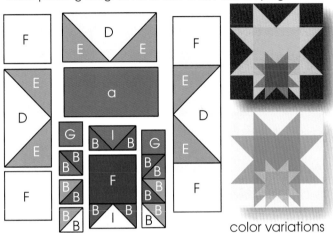

color variations

Me & My Shadow

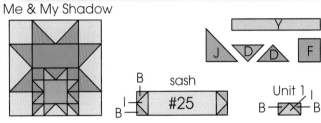

Patch Cutting for 6"–15" blocks on these two pages

Blk. Size:	6"	8"	9"	10"	12"	14"	15"
Block Patch	Cutting Dimensions for Patches						
D ⊠	4¼"	5¼"	5¾"	6¼"	7¼"	8¼"	8¾"
J ◻	3⅞"	4⅞"	5⅜"	5⅞"	6⅞"	7⅞"	8⅜"
I ⊠	2¾"	3¼"	3½"	3¾"	4¼"	4¾"	5"
E ◻	2⅜"	2⅞"	3⅛"	3⅜"	3⅞"	4⅜"	4⅝"
a ▭	2" x 3½"	2½" x 4½"	2¾" x 5"	3" x 5½"	3½" x 6½"	4" x 7½"	4¼" x 8"
F ▢	2"	2½"	2¾"	3"	3½"	4"	4¼"
B ◻	1⅝"	1⅞"	2"	2⅛"	2⅜"	2⅝"	2¾"
G ▢	1¼"	1½"	1⅝"	1¾"	2"	2¼"	2⅜"
Quilt Patch							
b ▢	3½"	4½"	5"	5½"	6½"	7½"	8"
#25 ▭	2" x 5"	2½" x 6½"	2¾" x 7¼"	3" x 8"	3½" x 9½"	4" x 11"	4¼" x 11¾"
Y ▭	1¼" x 6½"	1½" x 8½"	1⅝" x 9½"	1¾" x 10½"	2 x 12½"	2¼" x 14½"	2⅜" x 15½"

Notes

Mother & Child

For this block, I super-imposed a smaller Star of the Heartland, off center, over a larger one. Mother & Child pairs nicely with large or small Star of the Heartland blocks in a quilt. For superimposed stars, make sure the two stars contrast well.

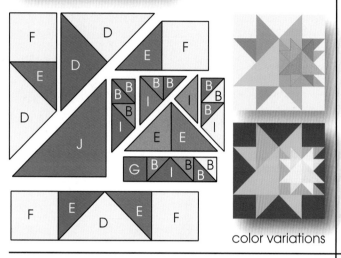

color variations

My Big Brother

For My Big Brother, I paired large and small Star of the Heartland stars once again. Here, the smaller star is positioned at the base of the block rather than at the side. Because the stars are asymmetrical, this block and the Mother & Child differ even when turned.

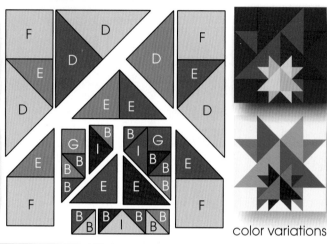

color variations

Double Puzzle

For this block, I paired large and small Green Bay Stars. To enhance the illusion of one star over the other, make the small star warmer and brighter than the large one. Turn the blocks in a quilt to play up the asymmetry. This block is not suitable for 9" and 15" block sizes.

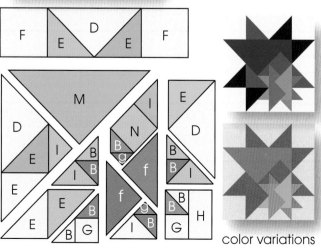

color variations

Like Father, Like Son

Here I combined large and small Branson Beauty stars. The block is similar to My Big Brother, though this one has three fewer pieces and appears layered rather than interlocked like the other.

color variations

Spring in the Air

I combined large and small Spring Picnic stars to create Spring in the Air. For the quilt at right, I set Spring in the Air blocks alternately with rectangles comprising a small Spring Picnic block joined to a similarly sized plain square.

Quilt piecing diagram and size chart are on page 101.

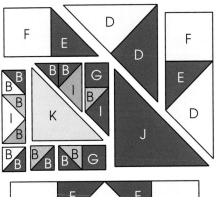

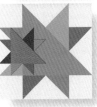

color variations

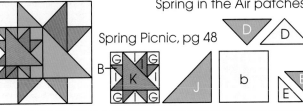

Spring in the Air

Spring Picnic can be made from Spring in the Air patches.

Spring Picnic, pg 48

Patch Cutting for 6"–15" blocks on these two pages

Blk. Size:	6"	8"	9"	10"	12"	14"	15"
Block Patch	Cutting Dimensions for Patches						
M ⊠	5¾"	7¼"	8"	8¾"	10¼"	11¾"	12½"
D ⊠	4¼"	5¼"	5¾"	6¼"	7¼"	8¼"	8¾"
J ◳	3⅞"	4⅞"	5⅜"	5⅞"	6⅞"	7⅞"	8⅜"
f ⊠	3½"	4¼"	4⅝"	5"	5¾"	6½"	6⅞"
K ◳	3⅛"	3⅞"	4¼"	4⅝"	5⅜"	6⅛"	6½"
I ⊠	2¾"	3¼"	3½"	3¾"	4¼"	4¾"	5"
E ◳	2⅜"	2⅞"	3⅛"	3⅜"	3⅞"	4⅜"	4⅝"
F ☐	2"	2½"	2¾"	3"	3½"	4"	4¼"
g ⊠	2"	2¼"	2⅜"	2½"	2¾"	3"	3⅛"
B ◳	1⅝"	1⅞"	2"	2⅛"	2⅜"	2⅝"	2¾"
N ☐	1½+"	1⅞+"		2¼"	2⅝"	3"	
G ☐	1¼"	1½"	1⅝"	1¾"	2"	2¼"	2⅜"
Quilt Patch							
b ☐	3½"	4½"	5"	5½"	6½"	7½"	8"

+ indicates a number halfway between the listed size and the next higher eighth inch.

Virginia Star

I designed Virginia Star in April, 2000 for my website. I combined elements of star and Virginia Reel blocks to achieve a new look. This star makes a perfect partner for a Virginia Reel block. Virginia Star cannot be made easily in 6" and 8" sizes.

color variations

Charlottesville Star

Charlottesville Star is a variation of my Virginia Star. In this version, the star points can contrast with the spirals rather than blending in as they do in Virginia Star. One block substitutes easily for the other one. Charlottesville Star is not suited for 6" and 8" blocks.

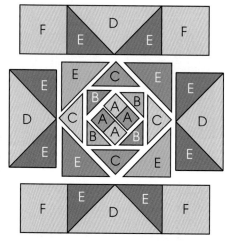

color variations

Virginia Reel

Virginia Reel is a popular traditional pattern. Typically, it is set with alternate plain squares or with blocks side by side. Blocks are turned so that light touches light and dark touches dark. I like to alternate Virginia Reels with stars for a unique quilt.

Quilt diagram and size chart are on page 102.

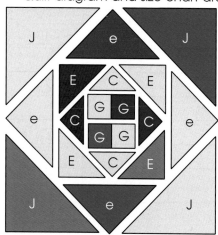

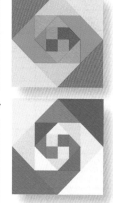

color variations

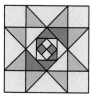

Charlotte Star   Virginia Reel

Virginia Star

Santa Barbara Star

I am partial to diagonals, as the two blocks on this page demonstrate. Santa Barbara Star was inspired by a Feathered Star. However, I feathered the interior of the star rather than the edges. While the inspiration was traditional, the new star looks sleekly modern.

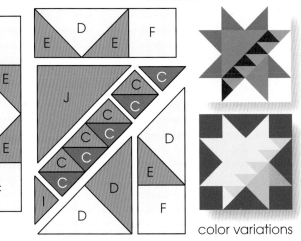

color variations

Fiery Star

This star resulted from my replacing the plain center square of an Evening Star with my Thunderstruck block from *Piece 'n' Play Quilts.* I love the way the block is divided in two with a zig-zag interface. A sawtooth border would be a fine complement to a quilt of Fiery Stars.

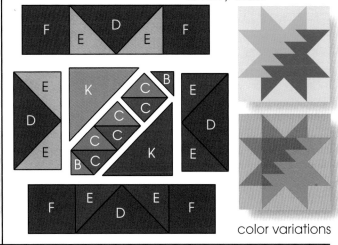

color variations

Patch Cutting for 6"–15" blocks on these two pages

Blk. Size:	6"	8"	9"	10"	12"	14"	15"
Block Patch	**Cutting Dimensions for Patches**						
D ⊠	4¼"	5¼"	5¾"	6¼"	7¼"	8¼"	8¾"
J ◨	3⅞"	4⅞"	5⅜"	5⅞"	6⅞"	7⅞"	8⅜"
K ◨	3⅛"	3⅞"	4¼"	4⅝"	5⅜"	6⅛"	6½"
e ◨	3"	3⅝+"	4+"	4⅜"	5⅛"	5¾+"	6⅛+"
I ⊠	2¾"	3¼"	3½"	3¾"	4¼"	4¾"	5"
E ◨	2⅜"	2⅞"	3⅛"	3⅜"	3⅞"	4⅜"	4⅝"
F ☐	2"	2½"	2¾"	3"	3½"	4"	4¼"
C ◨	1⅞+"	(use I)	2⅜+"	2⅝"	3"	(use I)	3½"
B ◨	1⅝"	1⅞"	2"	2⅛"	2⅜"	2⅝"	2¾"
G ☐	1¼"	1½"	1⅝"	1¾"	2"	2¼"	2⅜"
A ☐			1¼+"	1⅜"	1½+"	1¾"	1¾+"

C and I are the same size, different grain. Likewise, D and e are the same size, different grain.
+ indicates a number halfway between the listed size and the next higher eighth inch.

Notes

Chelsea Morning

This simple new star has a symmetrical block silhouette and star center, but it also has asymmetrical detailing. It coordinates well with the other star blocks in the Flying Stars family while making its own distinctive statement.

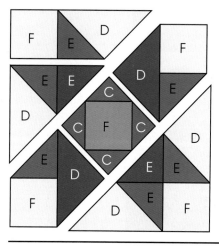

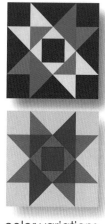

color variations

Walden Pond

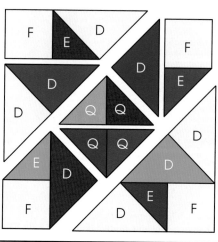

Walden Pond looks great in scraps or in just two fabrics. Note that the E and Q patches are the same size but have different grainlines. I make a distinction between them in order to have straight grain around the block edges and around its center.

color variations

Sea Breeze

Sea Breeze is a symmetrical variation for Chelsea Morning. I like the way the coloring at left appears to have layered blue triangles over same-sized ones of pink, orange, gold, and blue. This is accomplished by matching E and C triangles' colors.

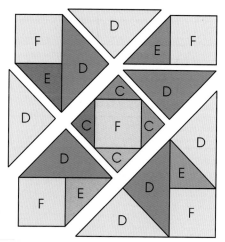

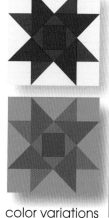

color variations

Seaside

Seaside is a new block in the traditional style. It would look great with a checkered border to match the block center. Another idea for a quilt would be to substitute Seaside and its block center for the Wishing Star block and center in the quilt on page 69.

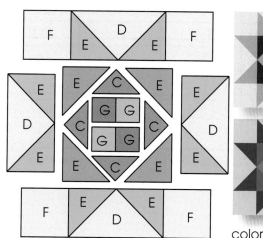

color variations

Wishing Star

Wishing Star is a new block that you can color with contrasting points to accentuate the vertical or color with blending points to minimize that effect. In the quilt at right, I repeated the block centers to make a pieced border.

Quilt piecing diagram and size chart are on page 102.

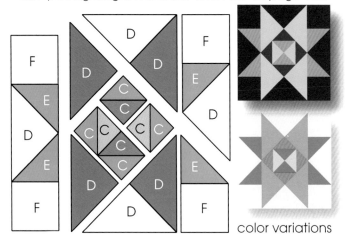

color variations

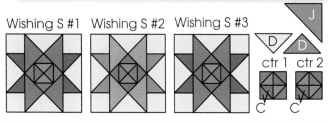

Wishing S #1   Wishing S #2   Wishing S #3

ctr 1   ctr 2

Patch Cutting for 6"–15" blocks on these two pages

Blk. Size:	6"	8"	9"	10"	12"	14"	15"
Block Patch	Cutting Dimensions for Patches						
D ⊠	4¼"	5¼"	5¾"	6¼"	7¼"	8¼"	8¾"
Q ⊠	3⅜"	4+"	4⅜+"	4¾"	5½"	6⅛+"	6½+"
I ⊠	2¾"	3¼"	3½"	3¾"	4¼"	4¾"	5"
E ◩	2⅜"	2⅞"	3⅛"	3⅜"	3⅞"	4⅜"	4⅝"
F □	2"	2½"	2¾"	3"	3½"	4"	4¼"
C ◩	1⅞+"	(use I)	2⅜+"	2⅝"	3"	(use I)	3½"
G □	1¼"	1½"	1⅝"	1¾"	2"	2¼"	2⅜"
Quilt Patch							
J ◩	3⅞"	4⅞"	5⅜"	5⅞"	6⅞"	7⅞"	8⅜"

C and I are the same size, different grain. Likewise, Q and E are the same size, different grain.
+ indicates a number halfway between the listed size and the next higher eighth inch.

Notes

Shooting Star

A trio of Flying Geese bursts diagonally through an Evening Star to make this new block. The geese can be colored to contrast or to blend with the star center for different effects. The geese add asymmetry and a strong diagonal element to the block.

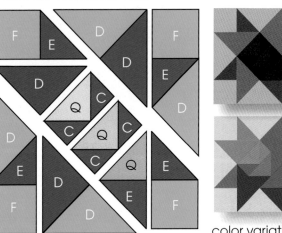

color variations

Comet Tails

Comet Tails is a new block reminiscent of a traditional Rambler. Here, though, one string of geese appears to cross over the other. I designed Comet Tails to continue the diagonal movement of Shooting Star in the quilt below.

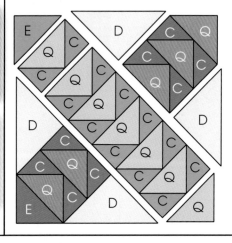

color variations

Star Flight

Star Flight is a simplification of Comet Tails, above right. I designed this block specifically to add variety to the quilt at right. Star Flight would also make an excellent border, with different looks for diagonal and straight sets.

Quilt diagram and size chart are on page 103.

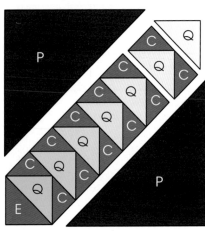

color variations

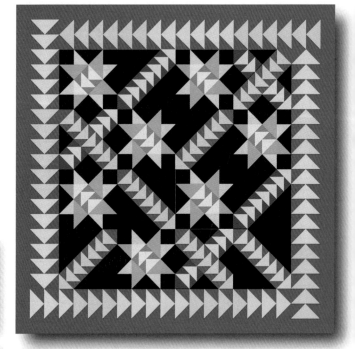

Shooting Star   Star Flight   Comet Tails

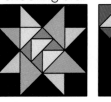

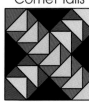

Unit 1

Wind in the Willows

I designed Wind in the Willows for this book, but it appeared first as a Block of the Moment on my website shortly before the book was published. It stands alone as a Pinwheel variation, or it can be set to form stars as in the quilt at right.

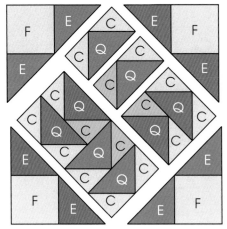

color variations

Wind in Willows

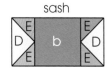

sash

Unit 1

Quilt piecing diagram and size chart are on page 103.

Patch Cutting for 6"-15" blocks on these two pages

Blk. Size:	6"	8"	9"	10"	12"	14"	15"
Block Patch	Cutting Dimensions for Patches						
P ◺	5⅜"	6⅞"	7⅝"	8⅜"	9⅞"	11⅜"	12⅛"
D ⊠	4¼"	5¼"	5¾"	6¼"	7¼"	8¼"	8¾"
Q ⊠	3⅜"	4+"	4⅜+"	4¾"	5½"	6⅛+"	6½+"
I ⊠	2¾"	3¼"	3½"	3¾"	4¼"	4¾"	5"
E ◺	2⅜"	2⅞"	3⅛"	3⅜"	3⅞"	4⅜"	4⅝"
F □	2"	2½"	2¾"	3"	3½"	4"	4¼"
C ◺	1⅞+"	(use I)	2⅜+"	2⅝"	3"	(use I)	3½"
Quilt Patch							
b □	3½"	4½"	5"	5½"	6½"	7½"	8"

C and I are the same size, different grain. Likewise, Q and E are the same size, different grain.
+ indicates a number halfway between the listed size and the next higher eighth inch.

Notes

Free Spirit

In *The Block Book*, I played with multiple staggered stars in one block. Here, I add a Nine-Patch. Free Spirit makes interesting secondary patterns in Log Cabin-type sets or makes a handsome border for a diagonally set quilt.

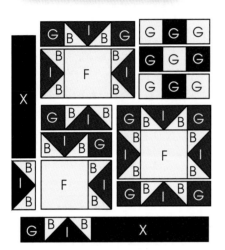

color variations

Free Spirit #1   Free Spirit #2

Quilt piecing diagram and size chart are on page 104.

Unit 1

Paul Revere's Ride

Paul Revere's Ride is a strongly directional block with its Flying Geese and parallel strips. It works well in a basket weave set as shown in the quilt at right. The Flying Geese and stars are singled out for the border and corner motifs.

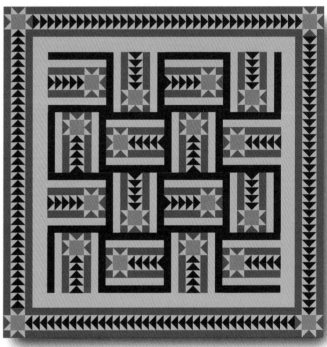

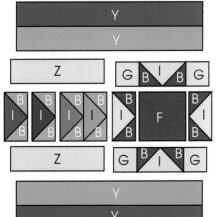

color variations

Paul Revere's

Quilt piecing diagram and size chart are on page 104.

Unit 1   Unit 2

Varsity Block

Though my Varsity Block is simpler, it looks similar to the traditional Snow Crystal block. The outer G, H, and I patches can be colored to contrast with the inner N and G patches to form an integral border. 10", 12" and 14" sizes are best suited for this block.

Sunshine State

Sunshine State combines Varsity Block with a Nine-Patch. It makes an ideal border for a diagonal quilt such as Varsity Medley on page 22. Four blocks (two each of opposite Nine-Patch colorings) make a handsome medallion center.

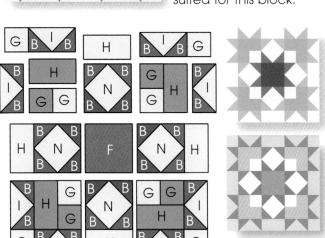

color variations

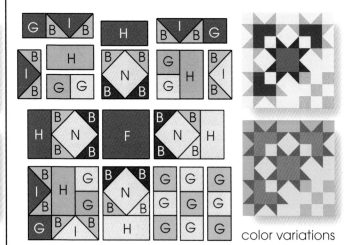

color variations

Patch Cutting for 8"–15" blocks on these two pages

Blk. Size:	8"	9"	10"	12"	14"	15"
Block Patch	Cutting Dimensions for Patches					
I ⊠	3¼"	3½"	3¾"	4¼"	4¾"	5"
F ☐	2½"	2¾"	3"	3½"	4"	4¼"
N ☐	1⅞+"		2¼"	2⅝"	3"	
B ◰	1⅞"	2"	2⅛"	2⅜"	2⅝"	2¾"
Y ☐	1½" x 8½"	1⅝" x 9½"	1¾" x 10½"	2 x 12½"	2¼" x 14½"	2⅜" x 15½"
X ☐	1½" x 5½"	1⅝" x 6⅛"	1¾" x 6¾"	2 x 8"	2¼" x 9¼"	2⅜" x 9⅞"
Z ☐	1½" x 4½"	1⅝" x 5"	1¾" x 5½"	2 x 6½"	2¼" x 7½"	2⅜" x 8"
H ☐	1½" x 2½"	1⅝" x 2¾"	1¾" x 3"	2" x 3½"	2¼" x 4"	2⅜" x 4¼"
G ☐	1½"	1⅝"	1¾"	2"	2¼"	2⅜"

+ indicates a number halfway between the listed size and the next higher eighth inch.

Notes

Three Sisters

I designed the blocks on this page as accents for other quilts. However, they can make interesting quilts on their own, creating a variety of secondary patterns depending on how you turn the blocks. The larger patches allow space to show off beautiful quilting.

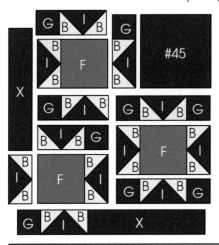

#45

color variations

Star in the Corner

Mix the Three Sisters and Star in the Corner blocks to make stars with irregular spacing. The larger spaces could feature big, beautiful prints if you don't care to quilt them elaborately. This block makes a good border block for a diagonally-set quilt.

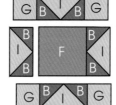

color variations

Checks in the Corner

This simple block can serve as an alternate block or border block to go with your favorite star blocks. I used it for one of the borders in the Varsity Medley quilt on page 22. It is also a natural for the Checkerboard and Free Spirit blocks (pages 76 and 72).

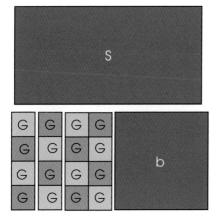

color variations

Checkered Stripe

This block would make a great border in a scrappy quilt set either straight or diagonally. In a small size, you can use Checkered Stripe to substitute for the usual block in a Rail Fence quilt. Use just two colors or a broad mix of scraps.

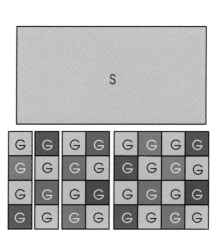

color variations

Night Flight

To create the Night Flight block, I surrounded a star with Flying Geese strips and Four-Patch corners. I set it with sashing in the quilt at right to keep the joints simple. This quilt would be handsome in plaids for a lodge look or in 19th century reproduction fabric.

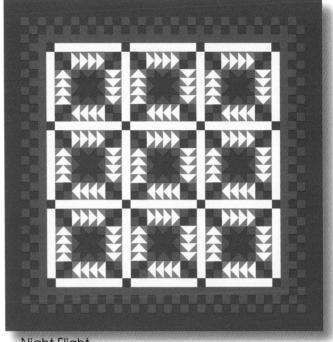

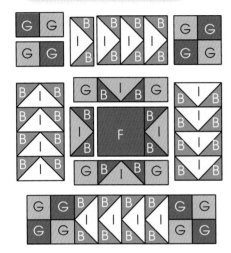

color variations

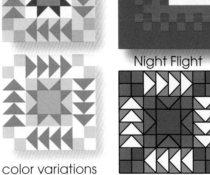

Night Flight

Quilt piecing diagram and size chart are on page 105.

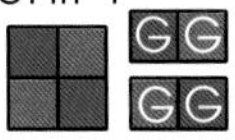

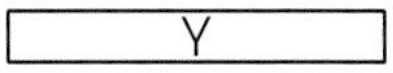

Unit 1

Y

Patch Cutting for 8"–15" blocks on these two pages

Blk. Size:	8"	9"	10"	12"	14"	15"
Block Patch	**Cutting Dimensions for Patches**					
S □	4½" x 8½"	5" x 9½"	5½" x 10½"	6½" x 12½"	7½" x 14½"	8" x 15½"
b □	4½"	5"	5½"	6½"	7½"	8"
#45 □	3½"	3⅞"	4¼"	5"	5¾"	6⅛"
I ⊠	3¼"	3½"	3¾"	4¼"	4¾"	5"
F □	2½"	2¾"	3"	3½"	4"	4¼"
B ◹	1⅞"	2"	2⅛"	2⅜"	2⅝"	2¾"
X □	1½" x 5½"	1⅝" x 6⅛"	1¾" x 6¾"	2 x 8"	2¼" x 9¼"	2⅜" x 9⅞"
G □	1½"	1⅝"	1¾"	2"	2¼"	2⅜"
Quilt Patch						
Y □	1½" x 8½"	1⅝" x 9½"	1¾" x 10½"	2 x 12½"	2¼" x 14½"	2⅜" x 15½"

Notes

Checkerboard

This simple block pairs well with the Rail Fence (right) or Gulf Coast (p. 57) blocks. Checkerboards are popular in country stylings, but the block would look quite contemporary in low-contrast batiks. I used it in Stars and Stripes Forever on page 44.

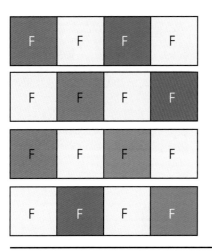

color variations

Rail Fence

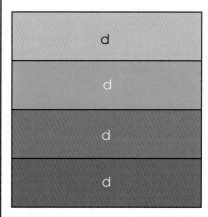

This is, perhaps, the simplest of quilt blocks. It is also one of the most versatile. Rail Fence can be used for borders, sashes, or in a variety of arrangements with like blocks. I use it for sashing in a Pinwheel quilt below.

color variations

Pinwheel

Pinwheel is an old favorite. It is often used for borders in English Medallion quilts. I use it for a border in my Twin-size Free Spirit Medley quilt. If you will press all joints clockwise in a block half, the joints will oppose for the final seam. Press the last seam open.

Cut J 2⅜" for 3" Pinwheel in the quilt on page 39.

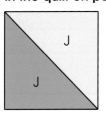
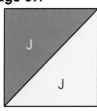
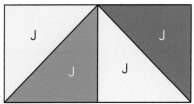
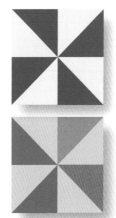

color variations

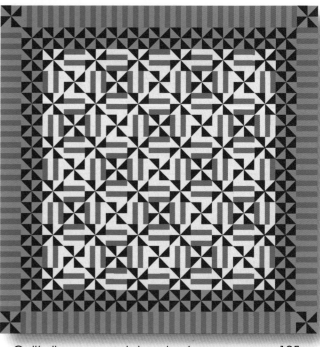

Quilt diagram and size chart are on page 105.

Pinwheel 1   Pinwheel 2   Rail Fence 1   Rail Fence 2

Dancing Pinwheels

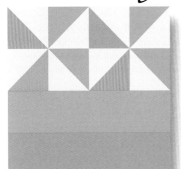

Dancing Pinwheels makes a boldly graphic statement in two strongly contrasting colors, as in the quilt at right. It looks simply charming in multicolored scraps. It makes a lovely border block or Rail Fence substitute.

Quilt diagram and size chart are on page 106.

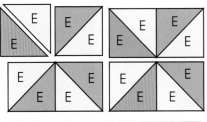

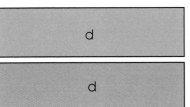

color variations

Dancing Pinwhl   corner block

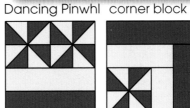

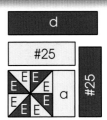

Patch Cutting for 5"–12" blocks on these two pages

Blk. Size*:	5"	6"	7"	8"	9"	10"	12"
Block Patch	**Cutting Dimensions for Patches**						
J ◻	3⅜"	3⅞"	4⅜"	4⅞"	5⅜"	5⅞"	6⅞"
E ◻	2⅛"	2⅜"	2⅝"	2⅞"	3⅛"	3⅜"	3⅞"
d ▭	1¾" x 5½"	2" x 6½"	2¼" x 7½"	2½" x 8½"	2¾" x 9½"	3" x 10½"	3½" x 12½"
F ▢	1¾"	2"	2¼"	2½"	2¾"	3"	3½"
Quilt Patch							
#25 ▭	1¾" x 4¼"	2" x 5"	2¼" x 5¾"	2½" x 6½"	2¾" x 7¼"	3" x 8"	3½" x 9½"
a ▭	1¾" x 3"	2" x 3½"	2¼" x 4"	2½" x 4½"	2¾" x 5"	3" x 5½"	3½" x 6½"

*Cutting for a 3" Pinwheel is listed below the Pinwheel block on page 76.

Notes

Americana

I designed Americana for my June, 2000, Block of the Moment. Use it to substitute for a Rail Fence block, or mix it with other blocks for a medley such as the one below right. It is a natural in red, white, and blue, but it is striking in rainbow colors, as well.

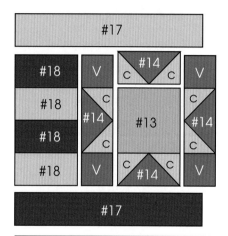

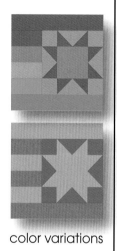

color variations

Potomac Pride

Potomac Pride is a versatile asymmetrical block. It plays well with star blocks, checkerboards, and Rail Fences. If you use it in a diagonal set, match the color sequence of stripes along the two edges, starting with a matched pair next to the Four-Patch.

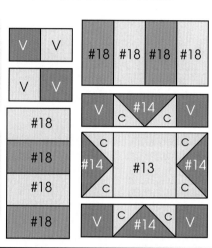

color variations

Liberty & Justice

Liberty & Justice is an orignial block with strong diagonal lines. Four of these blocks form the center of the quilt at right. Americana borders and Potomac Pride corners complete the quilt. Feel free to add to this for a spirited a medallion.

Quilt diagram and size chart are on page 106.

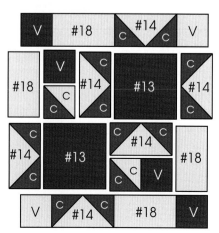

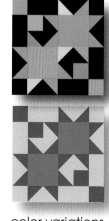

color variations

Liberty & Just   Americana   Potomac P

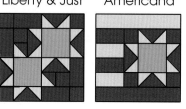

78   Americana Family

Bright Berry

Bright Berry combines elements of Weathervane and Ohio Star blocks. I like the way the additional points make the star shimmer. In the quilt at right, I paired the block with a chain that is like the Bright Berry block without the triangles.

Quilt diagram and size chart are on page 107.

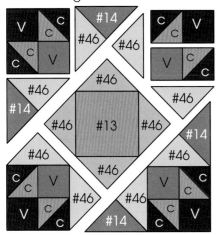

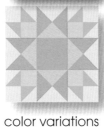

color variations

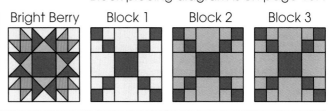

Block piecing diagram is on page 107.

Bright Berry   Block 1   Block 2   Block 3

Patch Cutting for 6"–15" blocks on these two pages

Blk. Size:	6"	7½"	9"	12"	15"
Block Patch	**Cutting Dimensions for Patches**				
#14 ⊠	3¼"	3¾"	4¼"	5¼"	6¼"
#13 ☐	2½"	3"	3½"	4½"	5½"
#46 ◩	2¼"	2⅝"	3"	3⅝+"	4⅜"
C ◨	1⅞"	2⅛"	2⅜"	2⅞"	3⅜"
#17 ☐	1½" x 6½"	1¾" x 8"	2" x 9½"	2½" x 12½"	3" x 15½"
#18 ☐	1½" x 2½"	1¾" x 3"	2" x 3½"	2½" x 4½"	3" x 5½"
V ☐	1½"	1¾"	2"	2½"	3"

+ indicates a number halfway between the listed size and the next higher eighth inch.
#14 and #46 are the same size, different grain.

Notes

America, the Beautiful

This is my son Will's design. It first appeared as a Block of the Moment in October, 2001. Later, I presented it as a quilt pattern in *Piece 'n' Play Quilts*. I simplified the block here by eliminating one set of stripes.

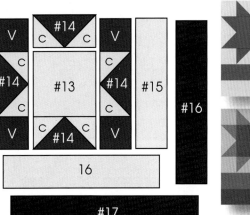

color variations

Ivanhoe

This new block is simply an Evening Star block surrounded by a saw-tooth (or feathered) border. It adds to the work, but it adds even more to the impact, especially when made from scraps. See how I adapted this block idea to make the quilt on page 40.

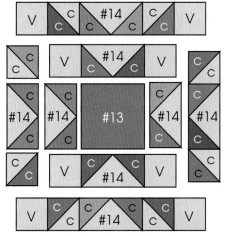

color variations

Night Lights

This block is just a basic star framed with rectangles. It coordinates with America, the Beautiful blocks. It works well in diagonal arrangements such as the one at right. Careful use of blending and contrast heighten the glowing effect.

Quilt diagram and size chart are on page 107.

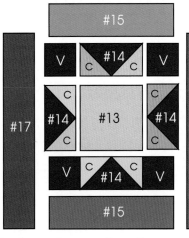

color variations

Patches #22 and #26 are shown on page 107.

America, Beaut #1 | America, Beaut #2 | America, Beaut #3 | Night Lights #1 | Night Lights #2

Game Night

Game Night is a basic star embellished. I show it with plain sashing at right, but it would also look good with star sashes to echo the star in the block center. A border of #10 squares on point would be suitable for such a quilt.

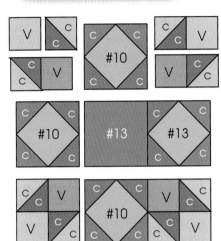

color variations

Game Night

Quilt piecing diagram and size chart are on page 108.

Unit 1

Patch Cutting for 6"–15" blocks on these two pages

Blk. Size:	6"	7½"	9"	12"	15"
Block Patch	**Cutting Dimensions for Patches**				
#14 ⊠	3¼"	3¾"	4¼"	5¼"	6¼"
#13 □	2½"	3"	3½"	4½"	5½"
#10 □	1⅞+"	2¼"	2⅝"	3¼+"	
C ◤	1⅞"	2⅛"	2⅜"	2⅞"	3⅜"
#17 ▭	1½" x 6½"	1¾" x 8"	2" x 9½"	2½" x 12½"	3" x 15½"
#16 ▭	1½" x 5½"	1¾" x 6¾"	2" x 8"	2½" x 10½"	3" x 13"
#15 ▭	1½" x 4½"	1¾" x 5½"	2" x 6½"	2½" x 8½"	3" x 10½"
V □	1½"	1¾"	2"	2½"	3"
Quilt Patch					
#22 ⊠	9¾"	11¾+"	13⅞+"	18¼"	22⅜+"
#26 ◤	9⅜"	11⅜+"	13½+"	17⅞"	22+"

+ indicates a number halfway between the listed size and the next higher eighth inch.

Notes

Jemima Puddleduck

I designed Jemima Puddleduck for the March, 2001 Block of the Moment. It was inspired by the Turkey Tracks block. The setting at right utilizes sashing strips on two sides of the block to stagger the blocks in the quilt.

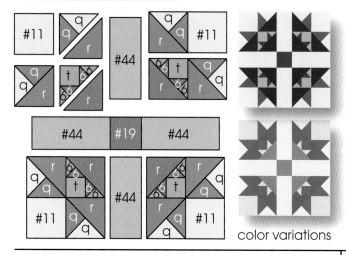

color variations

Jemima Puddle

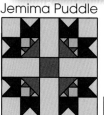

Quilt piecing diagram and size chart are on page 108.

#33

#31 #32

Thistledown

Blocks of this structure were traditionally made in sizes that were multiples of 5". I have included more sizes by changing proportions. In the 10", 15", and 20" sizes, #19 is the same size as #11. In other sizes, this is not the case.

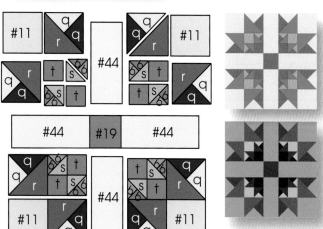

color variations

Rose Arbor

Rose Arbor is similar to Jemima Puddleduck. However, it has a clockwise spin to the larger points that the other block lacks. It would substitute beautifully for Jemima Puddleduck in the quilt above.

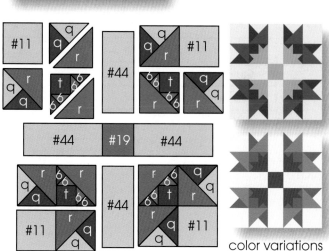

color variations

Summer Reading

Summer Reading is best made 10" or larger. In a smaller block, the #6 triangles finish at less than 1". Whenever you sew small patches to larger ones, as you do here, your seam allowances need to be not only consistent, but also accurate.

Celtic Chain

This block is a Double Irish Chain block reproportioned to suit the blocks in the Summer Fields family. It is used in the Summer Fields Sampler quilt on page 32. It looks most intriguing when the chain squares are in blending colors.

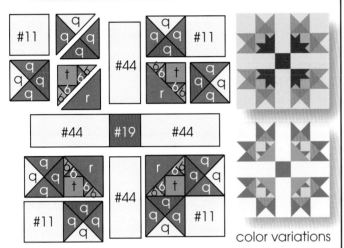

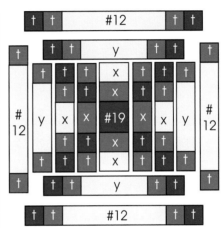

color variations

color variations

Patch Cutting for 8"–20" blocks on these two pages

Blk. Size:	8"	9"	10"	12"	14"	15"	20"
Block Patch	**Cutting Dimensions for Patches**						
q ⊠	3"	3¼"	3¼"	3¾"	4¼"	4¼"	5¼"
r ◺	2⅝"	2⅞"	2⅞"	3⅜"	3⅞"	3⅞"	4⅞"
#11 □	2¼"	2½"	2½"	3"	3½"	3½"	4½"
#6 ⊠	2⅛"	2¼"	2¼"	2½"	2¾"	2¾"	3¼"
s ◺	1¾"	1⅞"	1⅞"	2⅛"	2⅜"	2⅜"	2⅞"
#44 ▭	1½" x 4"	1½" x 4½"	2½" x 4½"	2½" x 5½"	2½" x 6½"	3½" x 6½"	4½" x 8½"
#19 □	1½"	1½"	2½"	2½"	2½"	3½"	4½"
#12 ▭	1⅜" x 5"	1½" x 5½"	1½" x 6½"	1¾" x 7½"	2" x 8½"	2" x 9½"	2½" x 12½"
y ▭	1⅜" x 3¼"	1½" x 3½"	1½" x 4½"	1¾" x 5"	2" x 5½"	2" x 6½"	2½" x 8½"
x ▭	1⅜" x 1½"	1½" x 1½"	1½" x 2½"	1¾" x 2½"	2" x 2½"	2" x 3½"	2½" x 4½"
† □	1⅜"	1½"	1½"	1¾"	2"	2"	2½"
Quilt Patch							
#33 ▭	2" x 3½"	2¼" x 4"	2½" x 4½"	3" x 5½"	3¼" x 6"	3½" x 6½"	4½" x 8½"
#32 ▭	1½" x 9½"	2" x 11"	2½" x 12½"	3½" x 15½"	3" x 17"	3½" x 18½"	4½" x 24½"
#31 ▭	1½" x 8½"	2" x 9½"	2½" x 10½"	3½" x 12½"	3" x 14½"	3½" x 15½"	4½" x 20½"

Some patches in this family remain the same size for different block sizes; x is a square in some sizes.

Turkey Tracks

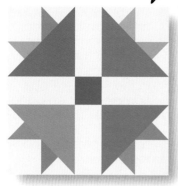

Turkey Tracks was one of the first traditional quilt blocks in my repertoire. It is simple to sew once you have mastered the perfect seam allowance. It has fewer pieces and a bit less detail than other blocks in the Summer Fields family.

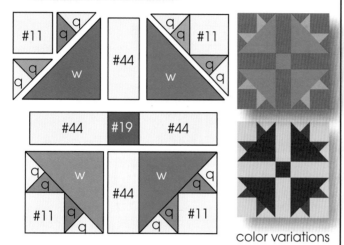

color variations

Breakfast at Tiffany's

This block's details look different depending on how you color them. (Compare the three color options on this page.) You could include multiple looks in one quilt. Breakfast at Tiffany's would look lovely in the Bayberry and Holly quilt setting shown on page 85.

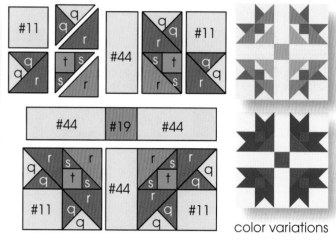

color variations

Summer Fields

This is the block for which I named the family. All blocks in the family have the same silhouette. Interior detail varies from block to block. This one looks good with blended colors or a multiplicity of scraps.

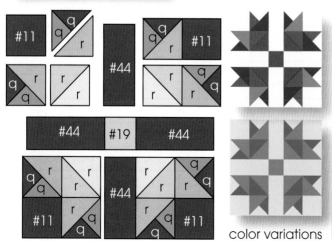

color variations

Guenevere

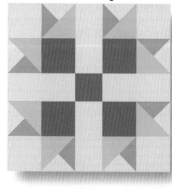

This new block looks almost floral when done in rose and green. Accentuate the green squares by repeating their color in alternating Celtic Chain blocks (page 83). Minimize the squares by matching them to the triangles as shown at bottom.

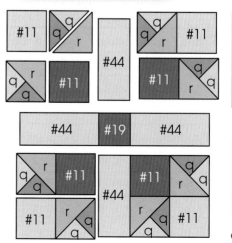

color variations

Bayberry & Holly

This is one of my simpler variations in the Summer Fields family. The triple sashes and Shoofly setting squares combine to make the elegant, traditional-looking quilt at right. To space the blocks generously, match the background to the wide outer sash strips.

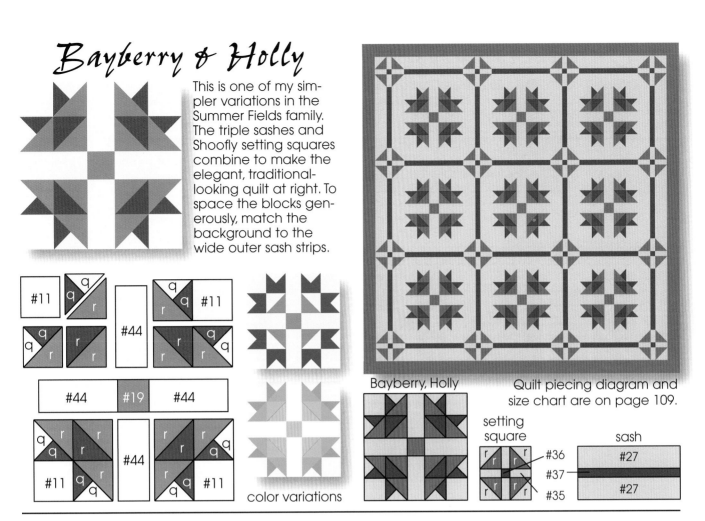

Bayberry, Holly

Quilt piecing diagram and size chart are on page 109.

color variations

setting square

sash

Patch Cutting for 8"–20" blocks on these two pages

Blk. Size:	8"	9"	10"	12"	14"	15"	20"
Block Patch	**Cutting Dimensions for Patches**						
w ◪	4⅜"	4⅞"	4⅞"	5⅞"	6⅞"	6⅞"	8⅞"
q ⊠	3"	3¼"	3¼"	3¾"	4¼"	4¼"	5¼"
r ◳	2⅝"	2⅞"	2⅞"	3⅜"	3⅞"	3⅞"	4⅞"
#11 ☐	2¼"	2½"	2½"	3"	3½"	3½"	4½"
s ◳	1¾"	1⅞"	1⅞"	2⅛"	2⅜"	2⅜"	2⅞"
#44 ☐	1½" x 4"	1½" x 4½"	2½" x 4½"	2½" x 5½"	2½" x 6½"	3½" x 6½"	4½" x 8½"
#19 ☐	1½"	1½"	2½"	2½"	2½"	3½"	4½"
t ☐	1⅜"	1½"	1½"	1¾"	2"	2"	2½"
Quilt Patch							
#27 ☐	2¼" x 8½"	2½" x 9½"	2½" x 10½"	3" x 12½"	3½" x 14½"	3½" x 15½"	4½" x 20½"
#37 ☐	1" x 8½"	1" x 9½"	1½" x 10½"	1½" x 12½"	1½" x 14½"	2" x 15½"	2½" x 20½"
#35 ☐	1" x 2¼"	1" x 2½"	1½" x 2½"	1½" x 3"	1½" x 3½"	2" x 3½"	2½" x 4½"
#36 ☐	1"	1"	1½"	1½"	1½"	2"	2½"

Some patches in this family remain the same size for different block sizes as proportions change slightly.

Christmas Goose

Christmas Goose was my November, 2002 Block of the Moment. In country, floral, or batik fabrics, it would make an attractive throw, table runner, or bed quilt. The Single Irish Chain blocks below pair well with Christmas Goose.

Quilt diagram and size chart are on page 109.

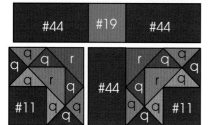 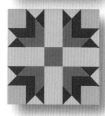

color variations

Christmas G   Single Irish C

#48   #47

Chain Edge B

unit 1   u2

11	11		2
11	11		2

Single Irish Chain

This is a traditional block used most often with alternating plain squares. Note that in my version, proportions may change with block size. That is why #11 and #19 are labeled differently, though they are alike in the size shown.

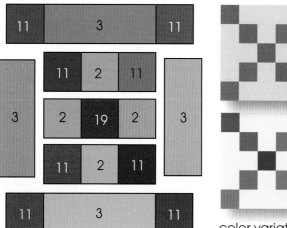 

color variations

Chain Edge Block

This rectangular block serves to complete the chains around the edge of the quilt shown above. These edge blocks alternate with #47 rectangles; #48 squares fill in at the quilt's corners.

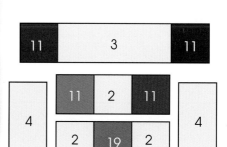 

color variations

Santa Fe Sunset

Santa Fe Sunset reminds me of the vivid colors of New Mexico. In the quilt at right, I accented the softer earth-and-sky colors with brilliant gold and a dash of chili pepper red for the small #6 triangles. The simple setting lets the glorious colors shine through.

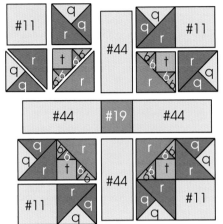

color variations

Santa Fe Sunset

Quilt piecing diagram and size chart are on page 110.

#30   19

Patch Cutting for 8"–20" blocks on these two pages

Blk. Size:	8"	9"	10"	12"	14"	15"	20"
Block Patch	**Cutting Dimensions for Patches**						
q ⊠	3"	3¼"	3¼"	3¾"	4¼"	4¼"	5¼"
r ◺	2⅝"	2⅞"	2⅞"	3⅜"	3⅞"	3⅞"	4⅞"
#3 ▭	2¼" x 5"	2½" x 5½"	2½" x 6½"	3" x 7½"	3½" x 8½"	3½" x 9½"	4½" x 12½"
#4 ▭	2¼" x 3¼"	2½" x 3½"	2½" x 4½"	3" x 5"	3½" x 5½"	3½" x 6½"	4½" x 8½"
#11 ▭	2¼"	2½"	2½"	3"	3½"	3½"	4½"
#6 ⊠	2⅛"	2¼"	2¼"	2½"	2¾"	2¾"	3¼"
#44 ▭	1½" x 4"	1½" x 4½"	2½" x 4½"	2½" x 5½"	2½" x 6½"	3½" x 6½"	4½" x 8½"
#2 ▭	1½" x 2¼"	1½" x 2½"	2½" x 2½"	2½" x 3"	2½" x 3½"	3½" x 3½"	4½" x 4½"
#19 ▭	1½"	1½"	2½"	2½"	2½"	3½"	4½"
t ▭	1⅜"	1½"	1½"	1¾"	2"	2"	2½"
Quilt Patch							
#47 ▭	5" x 8½"	5½" x 9½"	6½" x 10½"	7½" x 12½"	8½" x 14½"	9½" x 15½"	12½" x 20½"
#48 ▭	5"	5½"	6½"	7½"	8½"	9½"	12½"
#30 ▭	1½" x 8½"	1½" x 9½"	2½" x 10½"	2½" x 12½"	2½" x 14½"	3½" x 15½"	4½" x 20½"

Some patches in this family remain the same size for different block sizes as proportions change slightly. In some sizes, rectangle #2 is a square.

Sister's Star

Sister's Star, designed for my June, 2002, Block of the Moment, is the first block of the Shimmering Stars family. A Sister's Choice block is combined with an embellished star. Your coloring can bring out the cross, the star, or other elements.

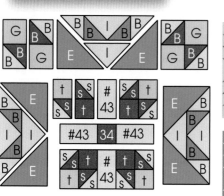

color variations

Bayfield Star

Here, the star center of Sister's Star is replaced with a Shoofly to make a slightly simpler block of the same family. In blocks having points around the edge, the points will be a quarter-inch in from the edge until after the block is sewn to the neighboring unit.

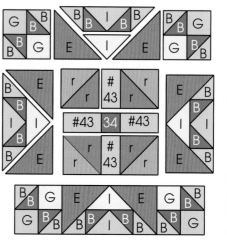

color variations

Over the River

Over the River has the same center as Sister's Star, but the block corners differ. Peace in Our Time, page 90, has the identical silhouette. All blocks on pages 88–95 have a similar scale and complexity, so they will go together even if the silhouettes differ slightly.

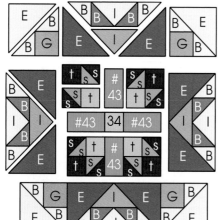

color variations

Quilt piecing diagram and size chart are on page 110.

Holiday Cheer

Holiday Cheer is an original block combining a Christmas Goose block center with a star and embellishments. Its silhouette matches that of Mom and Apple Pie, page 91. A monochromatic color scheme makes this star really shimmer, as you can see at right and below.

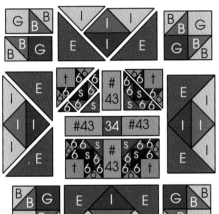

color variations

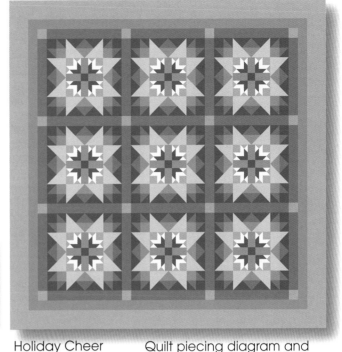

Holiday Cheer

Quilt piecing diagram and size chart are on page 111.

 Y   G

Patch Cutting for 10"–20" blocks on these two pages

Blk. Size:	10"	12"	14"	15"	18"	20"
Block Patch	**Cutting Dimensions for Patches**					
I ⊠	3¾"	4¼"	4¾"	5"	5¾"	6¼"
E ◺	3⅜"	3⅞"	4⅜"	4⅝"	5⅜"	5⅞"
r ◺	2⅞"	3⅜"	3⅞"	3⅞"	4⅝"	4⅞"
#6 ⊠	2¼"	2½"	2¾"	2¾"	3⅛"	3¼"
B ◺	2⅛"	2⅜"	2⅝"	2¾"	3⅛"	3⅜"
s ◺	1⅞"	2⅛"	2⅜"	2⅜"	2¾"	2⅞"
G ☐	1¾"	2"	2¼"	2⅜"	2¾"	3"
#43 ▭	1½" x 2½"	1½" x 3"	1½" x 3½"	2" x 3½"	2" x 4¼"	2½" x 4½"
† ☐	1½"	1¾"	2"	2"	2⅜"	2½"
#34 ☐	1½"	1½"	1½"	2"	2"	2½"
Quilt Patch						
D ⊠	6¼"	7¼"	8¼"	8¾"	10¼"	11¼"
J ◺	5⅞"	6⅞"	7⅞"	8⅜"	9⅞"	10⅞"
Y ▭	1¾" x 10½"	2" x 12½"	2¼" x 14½"	2⅜" x 15½"	2¾" x 18½"	3" x 20½"

Some patches in this family remain the same size for different block sizes as proportions change slightly.

Cottage in the Cotswolds

A stone cottage, a thatched roof, a country stroll that gives a glimpse of life in times long past: This memory suggested the name for my block. A simple star at the center radiates with layer upon layer of points. For a 12" block, replace #10 with four #9's and a V.

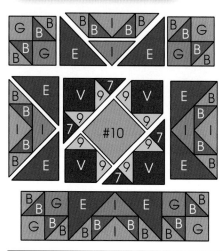

color variations

Peace in Our Time

The center of this block is like Bright Berry (page 79). The details beyond the green star are similar to Over the River (page 88). Complex blocks such as this can vary greatly with colorings that draw out different elements. This pattern is not suitable for a 10" block size.

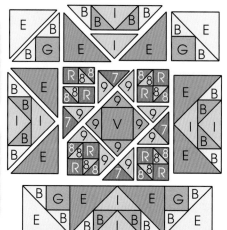

color variations

Kansas Summer

This original block recalls sunshine and sunflowers on a lazy afternoon. You can almost feel the heat in the radiating star points of the block. Kansas Summer does not make up well in the 10" block size.

Quilt diagram and size chart are on page 111.

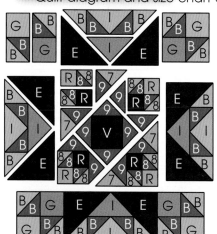

color variations

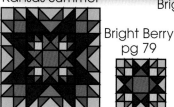

Kansas Summer

Bright Berry
pg 79

Bright Berry can be made like center of Kansas S.

#23
#21

b

Lakeside Cottage

Complex blocks such as this new one can look altogether different when you alter their coloring. That is part of the appeal. If you make the block larger than usual, your quilt will require fewer blocks and result in no extra work. Avoid the 10" size for this block.

Mom & Apple Pie

This original block just looks so American that I had to name it for Mom and apple pie. To keep a complex block from looking too busy, employ blending as well as contrast in the coloring. The 10" block size does not work well for this design variation.

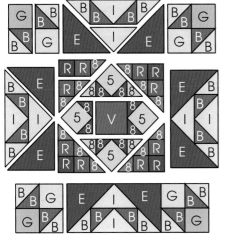

color variations

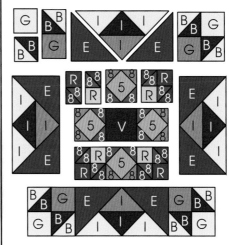

color variations

Patch Cutting for 10"–18" blocks on these two pages

Blk. Size:	10"	12"	15"	18"
Block Patch	**Cutting Dimensions for Patches**			
I ⊠	3¾"	4¼"	5"	5¾"
E ◻	3⅜"	3⅞"	4⅝"	5⅜"
#7 ⊠	2⅞"	3¼"	3¾"	4¼"
#10 ☐	2⅞"		4+"	4¾"
V ☐	2⅛+"	2½"	3"	3½"
B ◻	2⅛"	2⅜"	2¾"	3⅛"
#9 ◻	2+"	2¼"	2⅝"	3"
G ☐	1¾"	2"	2⅜"	2¾"
#5 ☐	1⅝+"	1⅞+"	2¼"	2⅝"
#8 ◻	1⅝+"	1⅞"	2⅛"	2⅜"
R ☐		1½"	1¾"	2"
Quilt Patch				
#23 ⊠	8¼+"	9¾"	11¾+"	13⅞+"
#21 ◻	7⅞+"	9⅜"	11⅜+"	13½+"
b ☐	5½"	7½"	8"	9½"

+ indicates a number halfway between listed size and next higher eighth inch.
#7 and #9 are the same size, different grain.

Home Field

I spend a good portion of each summer at the baseball field, watching my son play. I named this new block for our favorite place to view the team: our home field. Note the way the coloring changes the look of the block centers below.

color variations

Briar Rose

My daughter loves the princesses of fairy tales. I named this block for Briar Rose because the prickly triangles around this star reminded me of briars. The block is impressive in any colors you select.

color variations

Wimbledon Star

This block begins with a Moravian Star at its center. In the quilt at right, I mixed small Moravian Stars (page 52) with larger Wimbledon Stars for a fresh, new look. Show off your beautiful quilting in the b patches. Tennis, anyone?

Quilt diagram and size chart are on page 112.

color variations

Wimbledon Star

Moravian Star, pg 52

Moravian Star can be made from the same patches used in the Wimbledon center.

u1   unit 2

b

Old Mill Stream

I can almost hear the splash of the water and see the turning of the water wheel. The patches that surround this star can be colored in a variety of ways as shown at left and below. The two blocks on this page are closely related and interchangeable.

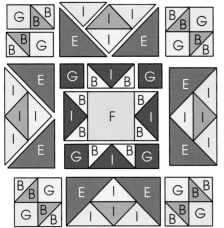

color variations

Country Store

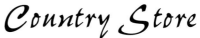

This block has an Amish look with its bright colors and black background. I can picture a country store in Kutztown or Kalona, with hand-made quilts hanging on the back wall. The block looks equally good in the spring tints or sunny hues below.

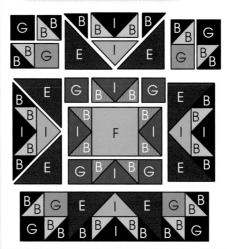

color variations

Patch Cutting for 10"–20" blocks on these two pages

Blk. Size:	10"	12"	14"	15"	18"	20"
Block Patch	Cutting Dimensions for Patches					
I ⊠	3¾"	4¼"	4¾"	5"	5¾"	6¼"
E ◩	3⅜"	3⅞"	4⅜"	4⅝"	5⅜"	5⅞"
F ☐	3"	3½"	4"	4¼"	5"	5½"
#67 ⊠	3"	3⅜"	3⅝+"	3⅞"	4⅜+"	4¾"
B ◩	2⅛"	2⅜"	2⅝"	2¾"	3⅛"	3⅜"
G ☐	1¾"	2"	2¼"	2⅜"	2¾"	3"
z ☐	1⅛" x 1¾"	1¼" x 2"	1⅜" x 2¼"	1⅜+" x 2⅜"	1⅝" x 2¾"	1¾" x 3"
i ☐	1⅛"	1¼"	1⅜"	1⅜+"	1⅝"	1¾"
Quilt Patch						
b ☐	5½"	6½"	7½"	8"	9½"	10½"

+ indicates a number halfway between the listed size and the next higher eighth inch.
Patches B and #67 are same size, different grain.

Notes

Exquisite Star

Exquisite Star was a Block of the Moment that I designed in March of 2002. For *Knockout Blocks and Sampler Quilts,* I designed the variations on these two pages. In each, a star or other motif is encircled by a 16-pointed star.

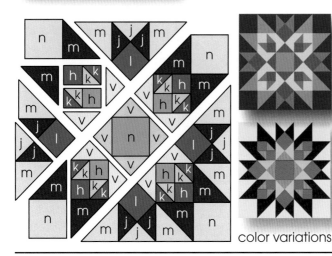

color variations

Ribbons & Bows

In the space between the Evening Star center and the 16 outer star points, this block has a ring of triangles that I colored to look like ribbons tied in bows (at left) and like Flying Geese (below). Make the block in either of these colorings or in your own.

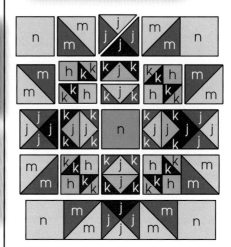

color variations

Liberty Belle

This block has a slightly different silhouette from the others on these two pages. I slid half of the 16 star points closer to the center for a new look. This shifts the emphasis from the outer ring of triangles to the middle ring.

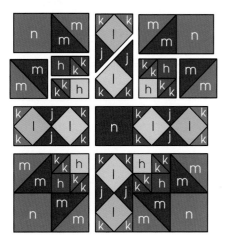

color variations

How Green Was My Valley

How Green Was My Valley is a new design featuring a star, a saw-tooth border, and another ring of star points. Combine the block with other blocks in the Exquisite Star family or with a Shimmering Star with a similar center, such as those on page 91.

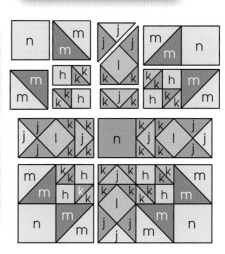

color variations

Tea for Two

This delightful block has the cheery warmth of a china teapot. In the flower-colored quilt at right, the block looks all dressed up for a tea party. The sashes and borders have a lacy delicacy that suits the blocks perfectly.

Quilt diagram and size chart are on page 112.

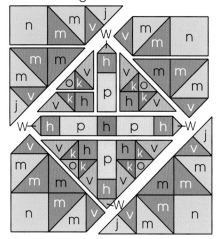

color variations

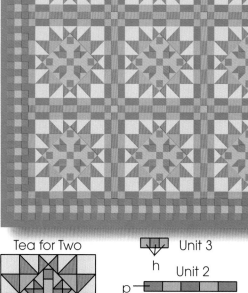

Tea for Two

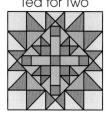

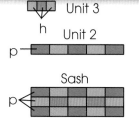

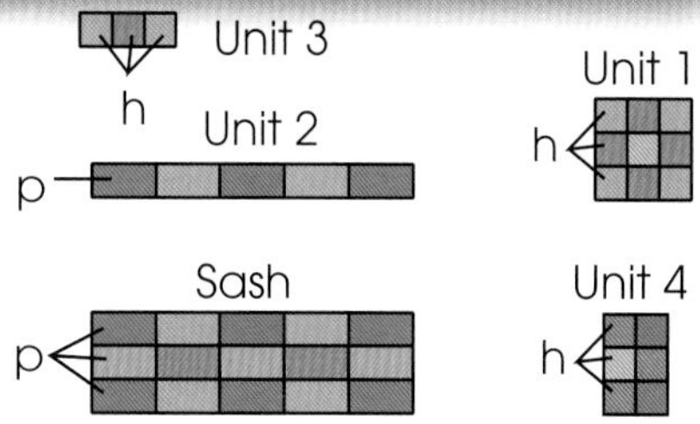

Patch Cutting for 10"–20" blocks on these two pages

Blk. Size:	10"	15"	20"
Block Patch	Cutting Dimensions for Patches		
j ⊠	3¼"	4¼"	5¼"
m ◺	2⅞"	3⅞"	4⅞"
o ⊠	2⅝"	3⅜"	4+"
n ☐	2½"	3½"	4½"
v ◺	2¼"	3"	3⅝+"
l ☐	1⅞+"	2⅝"	3¼+"
k ◺	1⅞"	2⅜"	2⅞"
W ◺	1½+"	1⅞+"	2¼"
p ▭	1½" x 2½"	2" x 3½"	2½" x 4½"
h ☐	1½"	2"	2½"

+ indicates a number halfway between the
listed size and the next higher eighth inch.
Patches k and o are the same size, different grain.
Likewise, j and v are the same size, different grain.

Quilt Diagrams and Size Charts

Chart lists finished length *or* width, including borders. Cut border the width listed; measure quilt for length.

Spring Picnic

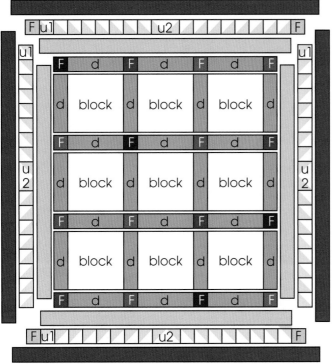

Bold entry in chart describes quilt as shown.

Spring Picnic Quilt (page 48)
Finished Quilt Measurements, with Borders

Block Size:	6"	8"	10"
# Blocks per Row			
3 blocks	**33"**	**44"**	**55"**
4 blocks	40½"	54"	67½"
5 blocks	48"	64"	80"
6 blocks	55½"	74"	92½"
7 blocks	63"	84"	105"
8 blocks	70½"	94"	117½"
9 blocks	78"	104"	
10 blocks	85½"	114"	
11 blocks	93"	124"	
12 blocks	100½"		
13 blocks	108"		
14 blocks	115½"		
cut borders	2"	2½"	3"

Pirouette

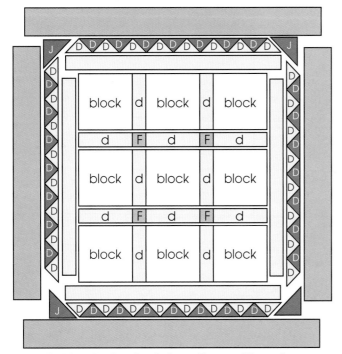

Bold entry in chart describes quilt as shown.

Pirouette Quilt (page 49)
Finished Quilt Measurements, with Borders

Block Size:	6"	8"	10"
# Blocks per Row			
3 blocks	**33"**	**44"**	**55"**
4 blocks	40½"	54"	67½"
5 blocks	48"	64"	80"
6 blocks	55½"	74"	92½"
7 blocks	63"	84"	105"
8 blocks	70½"	94"	117½"
9 blocks	78"	104"	
10 blocks	85½"	114"	
11 blocks	93"	124"	
12 blocks	100½"		
13 blocks	108"		
cut borders	2"	2½"	3"
	3½"	4½"	5½"

Green Bay Star

Bold entry in chart describes quilt as shown.

Green Bay Star Quilt (page 50)
Finished Quilt Measurements, with Borders

Block Size:	6"	9"	10"
# Blocks per Row*			
3 blocks	**34"**	**50⅞"**	**56½"**
4 blocks	42½"	63⅝"	70⅝"
5 blocks	51"	76¼"	84¾"
6 blocks	59½"	89"	98⅞"
7 blocks	68"	101¾"	113"
8 blocks	76½"	114⅜"	127¼"
9 blocks	85"	127⅛"	
10 blocks	93½"		
11 blocks	102"		
12 blocks	110½"		
13 blocks	119"		
14 blocks	127½"		
cut border	2⅝"	3⅝"	4"

*denotes number of large blocks across or down the center of the quilt

Moravian Star

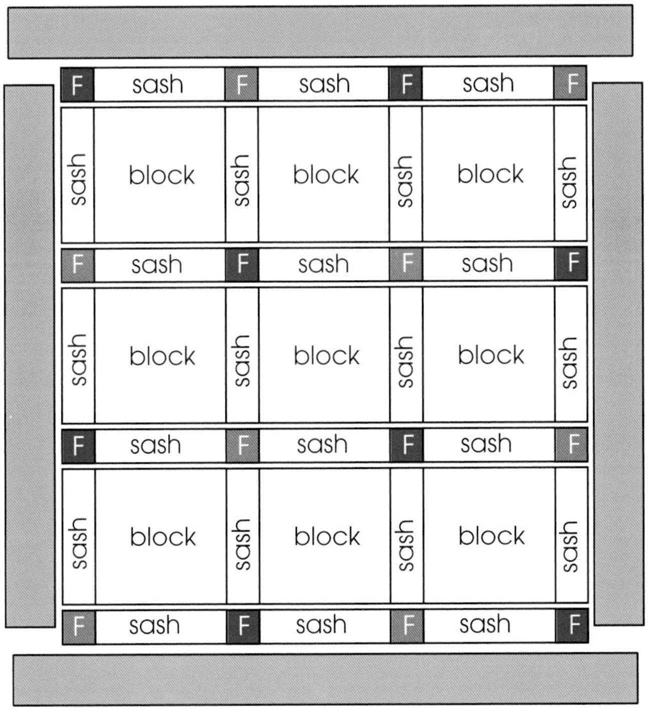

Bold entry in chart describes quilt as shown.

Moravian Star Quilt (page 52)
Finished Quilt Measurements, with Borders

Block Size:	6"	8"	10"
# Blocks per Row			
3 blocks	**28½"**	**38"**	**47½"**
4 blocks	36"	48"	60"
5 blocks	43½"	58"	72½"
6 blocks	51"	68"	85"
7 blocks	58½"	78"	97½"
8 blocks	66"	88"	110"
9 blocks	73½"	98"	122½"
10 blocks	81"	108"	
11 blocks	88½"	118"	
12 blocks	96"	128"	
13 blocks	103½"		
14 blocks	111"		
15 blocks	118½"		
cut border	2¾"	3½"	4¼"

Irish Star

Irish Star	Dublin Chain	Irish Star	Dublin Chain	Irish Star
Dublin Chain	Irish Star	Dublin Chain	Irish Star	Dublin Chain
Irish Star	Dublin Chain	Irish Star	Dublin Chain	Irish Star
Dublin Chain	Irish Star	Dublin Chain	Irish Star	Dublin Chain
Irish Star	Dublin Chain	Irish Star	Dublin Chain	Irish Star

border unit

Irish Star Quilt (page 54)
Finished Quilt Measurements, with Borders

Block Size:	9"	12"	15"
# Blocks per Row			
3 blocks	36"	48"	60"
5 blocks	**54"**	**72"**	**90"**
7 blocks	72"	96"	120"
9 blocks	90"	120"	
11 blocks	108"		
13 blocks	126"		
cut border	2¾"	3½"	4¼"

Bold entry in chart describes quilt as shown.

Mansfield Park

Block 5	Block 4	Block 3	Block 4	Block 5
Block 4	Mansfield Park	Block 2	Mansfield Park	Block 4
Block 3	Block 2	Mansfield Park	Block 2	Block 3
Block 4	Mansfield Park	Block 2	Mansfield Park	Block 4
Block 5	Block 4	Block 3	Block 4	Block 5

Bold entry in chart describes quilt as shown.

Mansfield Park Quilt (page 55)
Finished Quilt Measurements, with Borders

Block Size:	9"	12"	15"
# Blocks per Row*			
3 blocks	**36"**	**48"**	**60"**
5 blocks	54"	72"	90"
7 blocks	72"	96"	120"
9 blocks	90"	120"	
11 blocks	108"		
13 blocks	126"		

*denotes number of large blocks across or down the quilt. The number of blocks per row excludes edge blocks #3, 4, and 5, but these blocks are included in the quilt measurements.

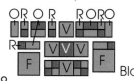
Block 3

Block 4

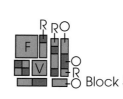
Block 5

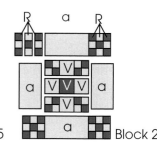
Block 2

Remembrance

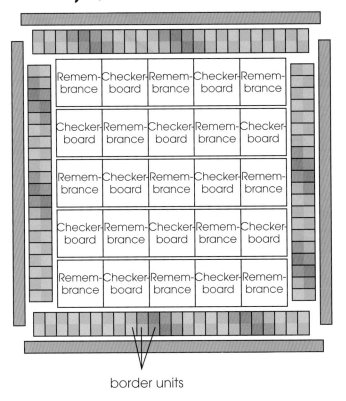

border units

Remembrance Quilt (page 56)
Finished Quilt Measurements, with Borders

Block Size:	6"	9"	12"
# Blocks per Row			
3 blocks	27"	40½"	54"
5 blocks	**39"**	**58½"**	**78"**
7 blocks	51"	76½"	102"
9 blocks	63"	94½"	126"
11 blocks	75"	112½"	
13 blocks	87"		
15 blocks	99"		
17 blocks	111"		
19 blocks	123"		
cut border	2"	2¾"	3½"

Bold entry in chart describes quilt as shown.

Rise Up So Early in the Morn

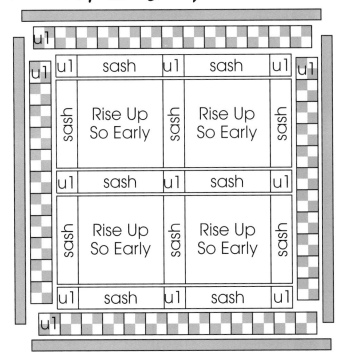

Rise Up So Early in the Morn Quilt (page 59)
Finished Quilt Measurements, with Borders

Block Size:	8"	10"	12"
# Blocks per Row			
1 block	18"	22½"	27"
2 blocks	**28"**	**35"**	**42"**
3 blocks	38"	47½"	57"
4 blocks	48"	60"	72"
5 blocks	58"	72½"	87"
6 blocks	68"	85"	102"
7 blocks	78"	97½"	117"
8 blocks	88"	110"	
9 blocks	98"	122½"	
10 blocks	108"		
11 blocks	118"		
cut border	1½"	1¾"	2"

Bold entry in chart describes quilt as shown.

Woodworker's Puzzle

Bold entry in chart describes quilt as shown.

Woodworker's Puzzle Quilt (page 61)
Finished Quilt Measurements, with Borders

Block Size:	10"	12"	14"
# Blocks per Row*			
1 block	33¼"	40"	46⅝"
2 blocks	**54½"**	**65⅜"**	**76¼"**
3 blocks	75¾"	90⅞"	106"
4 blocks	96⅞"	116¼"	
5 blocks	118⅛"		
cut border	3"	3½"	4"

*denotes number of large blocks across or down the center of the quilt

Pacific Star

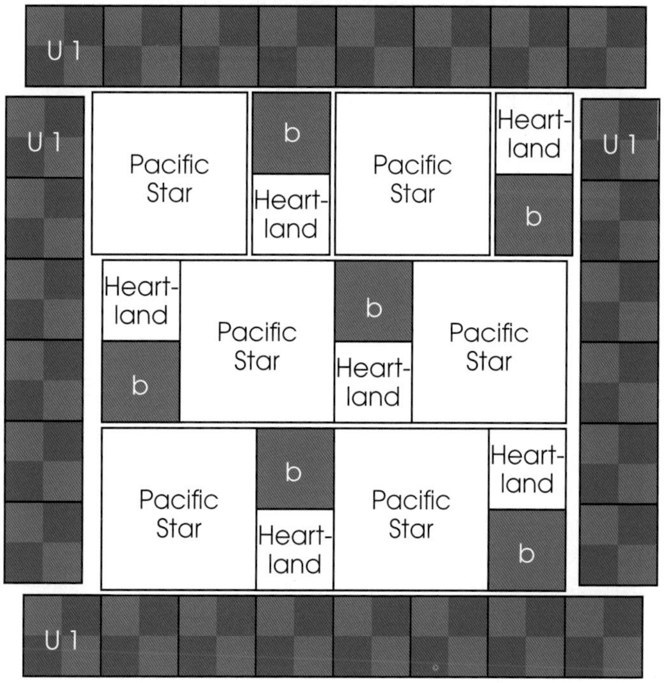

Bold entry in chart describes quilt as shown.

Add to length in one-block increments; add to width in one-and-one-half block increments. Blocks per row are labeled "w" for rows suitable for width and "l" for rows suitable for length. (The quilt can be turned sideways, if desired, with l and w switched.)

Pacific Star Quilt (page 62)
Finished Quilt Measurements, with Borders

Block Size:	10"	12"	14"
# Blocks per Row**			
1½ blocks (w)	25"	30"	35"
2 blocks (l)	30"	36"	42"
3 blocks (l, w)	**40"**	**48"**	**56"**
4 blocks (l)	50"	60"	70"
4½ blocks (w)	55"	66"	77"
5 blocks (l)	60"	72"	84"
6 blocks (l, w)	70"	84"	98"
7 blocks (l)	80"	96"	112"
7½ blocks (w)	85"	102"	119"
8 blocks (l)	90"	108"	126"
9 blocks (l, w)	100"	120"	
10 blocks (l)	110"		
10½ blocks (w)	115"		

**denotes the number of large blocks (or the equivalent distance) per row, with a small block covering half the distance of a large block

100

Me & My Shadow

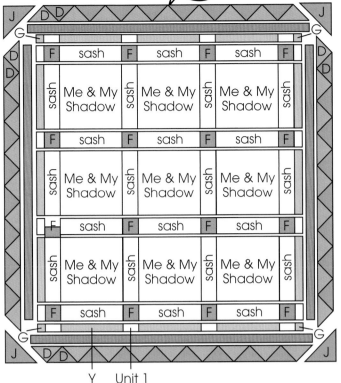

Y   Unit 1

Me & My Shadow Quilt (page 63)
Finished Quilt Measurements, with Borders

Block Size:	10"	12"	14"
# Blocks per Row			
1 block	25"	30"	35"
2 blocks	37½"	45"	52½"
3 blocks	**50"**	**60"**	**70"**
4 blocks	62½"	75"	87½"
5 blocks	75"	90"	105"
6 blocks	87½"	105"	122½"
7 blocks	100"	120"	
8 blocks	112½"		
9 blocks	125"		
cut border	1¾"	2"	2¼"

Bold entry in chart describes quilt as shown.

Spring in the Air

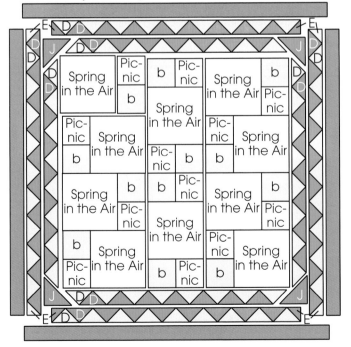

Bold entry in chart describes quilt as shown.

Add to length in two-block increments; add to width in one-and-one-half block increments alternated with one-block increments. Blocks per row are labeled "w" for rows suitable for width and "l" for rows suitable for length. (Turn quilt sideways, if desired.)

Spring in the Air Quilt (page 65)
Finished Quilt Measurements, with Borders

Block Size:	10"	12"	14"
# Blocks per Row**			
1½ blocks (w)	30"	36"	42"
2 blocks (l)	35"	42"	49"
2½ blocks (w)	40	48"	56"
4 blocks (l, w)	**55"**	**66"**	**77"**
5 blocks (w)	65"	78"	91"
6 blocks (l)	75"	90"	105"
6½ blocks (w)	80"	96"	112"
7½ blocks (w)	90"	108"	126"
8 blocks (l)	95"	114"	
9 blocks (w)	105"	126"	
10 blocks (l, w)	115"		
cut border	3"	3½"	4"

**denotes the number of large blocks (or the equivalent distance) per row, with a small block covering half the distance of a large block

Virginia Reel

Char-lottes-ville Star	Virginia Reel	Char-lottes-ville Star	Virginia Reel	Char-lottes-ville Star
Virginia Reel	Virginia Star	Virginia Reel	Virginia Star	Virginia Reel
Char-lottes-ville Star	Virginia Reel	Char-lottes-ville Star	Virginia Reel	Char-lottes-ville Star
Virginia Reel	Virginia Star	Virginia Reel	Virginia Star	Virginia Reel
Char-lottes-ville Star	Virginia Reel	Char-lottes-ville Star	Virginia Reel	Char-lottes-ville Star

Virginia Reel Quilt (page 66)
Finished Quilt Measurements, with Borders

Block Size:	10"	12"	15"
# Blocks per Row			
3 blocks	35"	42"	52½"
5 blocks	**55"**	**66"**	**82½"**
7 blocks	75"	90"	112½"
9 blocks	95"	114"	
11 blocks	115"		
cut border	3"	3½"	4¼"

Bold entry in chart describes quilt as shown.

Wishing Star

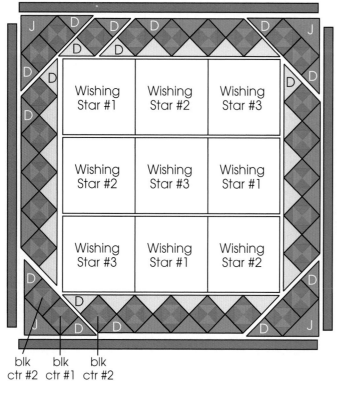

blk ctr #2   blk ctr #1   blk ctr #2

Bold entry in chart describes quilt as shown.

Wishing Star Quilt (page 69)
Finished Quilt Measurements, with Borders

Block Size:	8"	10"	12"
# Blocks per Row			
1 block	18"	22½"	27"
2 blocks	26"	32½"	39"
3 blocks	**34"**	**42½"**	**51"**
4 blocks	42"	52½"	63"
5 blocks	50"	62½"	75"
6 blocks	58"	72½"	87"
7 blocks	66"	82½"	99"
8 blocks	74"	92½"	111"
9 blocks	82"	102½"	123"
10 blocks	90"	112½"	
11 blocks	98"	122½"	
12 blocks	106"		
13 blocks	114"		
14 blocks	122"		
cut border	1½"	1¾"	2"

Star Flight

Bold entry in chart describes quilt as shown.

Star Flight Quilt (page 70)
Finished Quilt Measurements, with Borders

Block Size:	8"	10"	12"
# Blocks per Row			
2 blocks	28"	35"	42"
3 blocks	36"	45"	54"
4 blocks	**44"**	**55"**	**66"**
5 blocks	52"	65"	78"
6 blocks	60"	75"	90"
7 blocks	68"	85"	102"
8 blocks	76"	95"	114"
9 blocks	84"	105"	126"
10 blocks	92"	115"	
11 blocks	100"	125"	
12 blocks	108"		
13 blocks	116"		
14 blocks	124"		
cut border	2½"	3"	3½"

Wind in the Willows

Bold entry in chart describes quilt as shown.

Wind in the Willows Quilt (page 71)
Finished Quilt Measurements, with Borders

Block Size:	8"	10"	12"
# Blocks per Row			
2 blocks	32"	40"	48"
3 blocks	**44"**	**55"**	**66"**
4 blocks	56"	70"	84"
5 blocks	68"	85"	102"
6 blocks	80"	100"	120"
7 blocks	92"	115"	
8 blocks	104"		
9 blocks	116"		
10 blocks	128"		
cut border	2½"	3"	3½"

*denotes number of Wind in the Willows blocks across or down the center of the quilt

Free Spirit

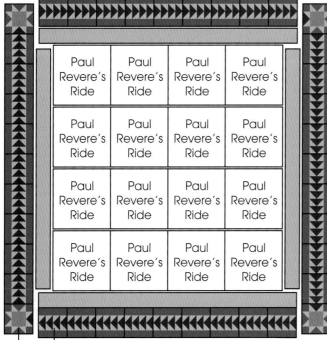

After joining Free Spirit blocks in three rows of three, add borders in sequence listed in pink.

Free Spirit Quilt (page 72)
Finished Quilt Measurements, with Borders

Block Size:	8"	12"	14"
# Blocks per Row			
2 blocks	32"	48"	56"
3 blocks	**40"**	**60"**	**70"**
4 blocks	48"	72"	84"
5 blocks	56"	84"	98"
6 blocks	64"	96"	112"
7 blocks	72"	108"	126"
8 blocks	80"	120"	
9 blocks	88"		
10 blocks	96"		
11 blocks	104"		
12 blocks	112"		
13 blocks	120"		
cut border	6½"	9½"	11"

Bold entry in chart describes quilt as shown.

Paul Revere's Ride

unit 2 unit 1

Paul Revere Quilt (page 72)
Finished Quilt Measurements, with Borders

Block Size:	8"	12"	14"
# Blocks per Row			
2 blocks	28"	42"	49"
3 blocks	36"	54"	63"
4 blocks	**44"**	**66"**	**77"**
5 blocks	52"	78"	91"
6 blocks	60"	90"	105"
7 blocks	68"	102"	119"
8 blocks	76"	114"	
9 blocks	84"	126"	
10 blocks	92"		
11 blocks	100"		
12 blocks	108"		
13 blocks	116"		
14 blocks	124"		
cut border	2½"	3½"	4"

Bold entry in chart describes quilt as shown.

Night Flight

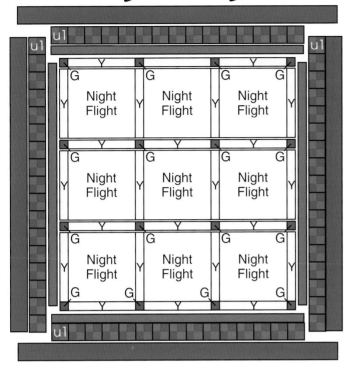

Night Flight Quilt (page 75)
Finished Quilt Measurements, with Borders

Block Size:	10"	12"	14"
# Blocks per Row			
1 block	25"	30"	35"
2 blocks	36¼"	43½"	50¾"
3 blocks	**47½"**	**57"**	**66½"**
4 blocks	58¾"	70½"	82¼"
5 blocks	70"	84"	98"
6 blocks	81¼"	97½"	113¾"
7 blocks	92½"	111"	129½"
8 blocks	103¾"	124½"	
9 blocks	115"		
10 blocks	126¼"		
cut borders	1¾"	2"	2¼"
	3"	3½"	4"

Bold entry in chart describes quilt as shown.

Pinwheel

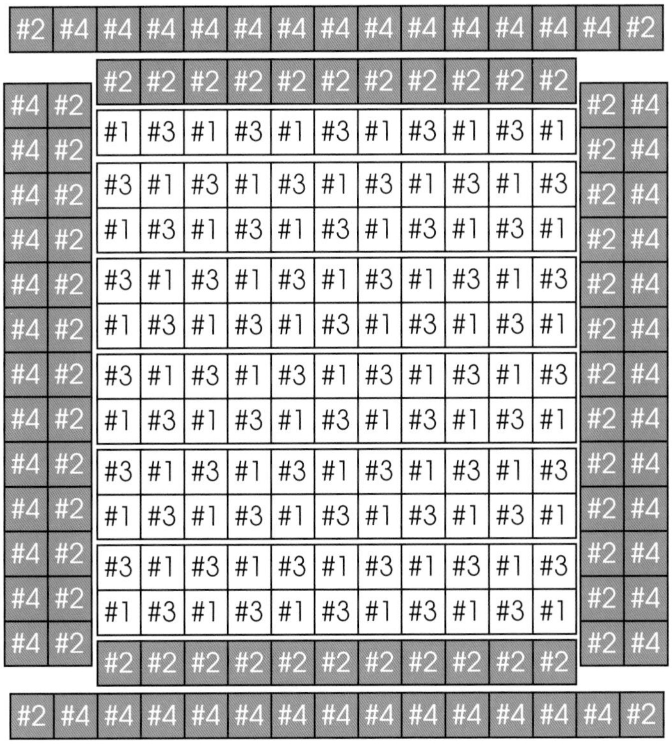

#2	#4	#4	#4	#4	#4	#4	#4	#4	#4	#4	#4	#4	#4	#2
#4	#2	#2	#2	#2	#2	#2	#2	#2	#2	#2	#2	#2	#2	#4
#4	#2	#1	#3	#1	#3	#1	#3	#1	#3	#1	#3	#1	#2	#4
#4	#2	#3	#1	#3	#1	#3	#1	#3	#1	#3	#1	#3	#2	#4
#4	#2	#1	#3	#1	#3	#1	#3	#1	#3	#1	#3	#1	#2	#4
#4	#2	#3	#1	#3	#1	#3	#1	#3	#1	#3	#1	#3	#2	#4
#4	#2	#1	#3	#1	#3	#1	#3	#1	#3	#1	#3	#1	#2	#4
#4	#2	#3	#1	#3	#1	#3	#1	#3	#1	#3	#1	#3	#2	#4
#4	#2	#1	#3	#1	#3	#1	#3	#1	#3	#1	#3	#1	#2	#4
#4	#2	#3	#1	#3	#1	#3	#1	#3	#1	#3	#1	#3	#2	#4
#4	#2	#1	#3	#1	#3	#1	#3	#1	#3	#1	#3	#1	#2	#4
#4	#2	#3	#1	#3	#1	#3	#1	#3	#1	#3	#1	#3	#2	#4
#4	#2	#1	#3	#1	#3	#1	#3	#1	#3	#1	#3	#1	#2	#4
#4	#2	#2	#2	#2	#2	#2	#2	#2	#2	#2	#2	#2	#2	#4
#2	#4	#4	#4	#4	#4	#4	#4	#4	#4	#4	#4	#4	#4	#2

Bold entry in chart describes quilt as shown.

Pinwheel & Rail Fence Quilt (page 76)
Finished Quilt Measurements, with Borders

Block Size:	5"	6"	8"
# Blocks per Row*			
1 block	25"	30"	40"
3 blocks	35"	42"	56"
5 blocks	45"	54"	72"
7 blocks	55"	66"	88"
9 blocks	65"	78"	104"
11 blocks	**75"**	**90"**	**120"**
13 blocks	85"	102"	
15 blocks	95"	114"	
17 blocks	105"	126"	
19 blocks	115"		
21 blocks	125"		

*denotes number of #1 and #3 blocks across or down the quilt center

Dancing Pinwheels

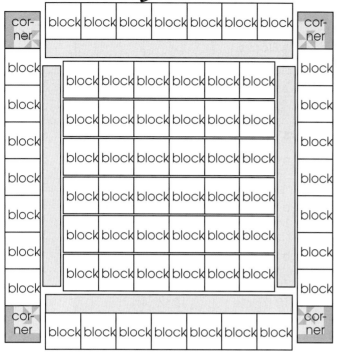

Bold entry in chart describes quilt as shown.

Dancing Pinwheel Quilt (page 77)
Finished Quilt Measurements, with Borders

Block Size:	6"	8"	10"
# Blocks per Row*			
4 blocks	42"	56"	70"
5 blocks	48"	64"	80"
6 blocks	**54"**	**72"**	**90"**
7 blocks	60"	80"	100"
8 blocks	66"	88"	110"
9 blocks	72"	96"	120"
10 blocks	78"	104"	130"
11 blocks	84"	112"	
12 blocks	90"	120"	
13 blocks	96"	128"	
14 blocks	102"		
15 blocks	108"		
16 blocks	114"		
cut border	3½"	4½"	5½"

*denotes number of blocks in a row in the quilt center, inside the plain border

Liberty & Justice

Potomac Pride	Ameri-cana	Ameri-cana	Ameri-cana	Potomac Pride
Ameri-cana				Ameri-cana
Ameri-cana		Liberty & Justice	Liberty & Justice	Ameri-cana
Ameri-cana		Liberty & Justice	Liberty & Justice	Ameri-cana
Potomac Pride	Ameri-cana	Ameri-cana	Ameri-cana	Potomac Pride

Bold entry in chart describes quilt as shown.

Liberty & Justice Quilt (page 78)
Finished Quilt Measurements, with Borders

Block Size:	9"	12"	15"
# Blocks per Row**			
5 blocks	**45"**	**60"**	**75"**
7 blocks	63"	84"	105"
9 blocks	81"	108"	
11 blocks	99"		
13 blocks	117"		
cut border	5"	6½"	8"

**denotes number of blocks across or down the *outside* edge of the quilt

Bright Berry

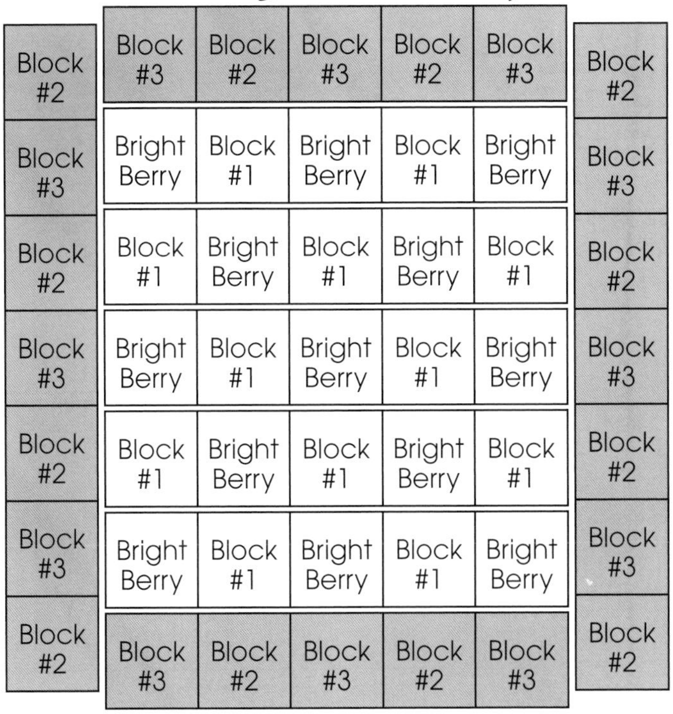

Block #2	Block #3	Block #2	Block #3	Block #2	Block #3	Block #2
Block #3	Bright Berry	Block #1	Bright Berry	Block #1	Bright Berry	Block #3
Block #2	Block #1	Bright Berry	Block #1	Bright Berry	Block #1	Block #2
Block #3	Bright Berry	Block #1	Bright Berry	Block #1	Bright Berry	Block #3
Block #2	Block #1	Bright Berry	Block #1	Bright Berry	Block #1	Block #2
Block #3	Bright Berry	Block #1	Bright Berry	Block #1	Bright Berry	Block #3
Block #2	Block #3	Block #2	Block #3	Block #2	Block #3	Block #2

Bold entry in chart describes quilt as shown.

Bright Berry Quilt (page 79)
Finished Quilt Measurements, with Borders

Block Size:	7½"	9"	12"
# Blocks per Row*			
1 block	22½"	27"	36"
3 blocks	37½"	45"	60"
5 blocks	**52½"**	**63"**	**84"**
7 blocks	67½"	81"	108"
9 blocks	82½"	99"	
11 blocks	97½"	117"	
13 blocks	112½"		
15 blocks	127½"		

*denotes number of blocks across or down the quilt center, inside the purple #2 and #3 blocks.

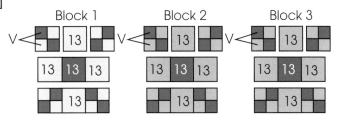

Block 1   Block 2   Block 3

Night Lights

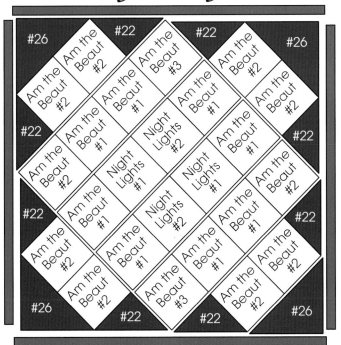

Bold entry in chart describes quilt as shown.

Night Lights (page 80)
Finished Quilt Measurements, with Borders

Block Size:	7½"	9"	12"
# Blocks per Row**			
4 blocks	**45"**	**53⅞"**	**71⅞"**
6 blocks	66⅛"	79¾"	105⅞"
8 blocks	87⅜"	104⅞"	
10 blocks	108⅝"		
cut border	**1¾"**	**2"**	**2½"**

**denotes number of blocks across or down the center of the quilt

107

Game Night

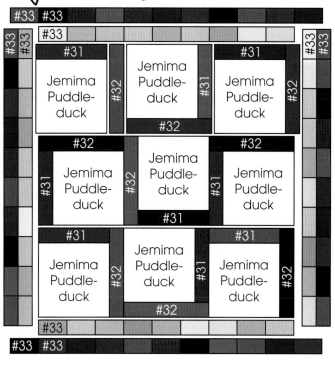

Block Size:	7½"	9"	12"
# Blocks per Row			
3 blocks	**32½"**	**39"**	**52"**
4 blocks	41¼"	49½"	66"
5 blocks	50"	60"	80"
6 blocks	58¾"	70½"	94"
7 blocks	67½"	81"	108"
8 blocks	76¼"	91½"	122"
9 blocks	85"	102"	
10 blocks	93¾"	112½"	
11 blocks	102½"	123"	
12 blocks	111¼"		
13 blocks	120"		
14 blocks	128¾"		

Bold entry in chart describes quilt as shown.

Jemima Puddleduck

Jemima Puddleduck Quilt (page 82)
Finished Quilt Measurements, with Borders

Block Size:	10"	12"	14"
# Blocks per Row			
2 blocks	32"	40"	44"
3 blocks	**44"**	**55"**	**60½"**
4 blocks	56"	70"	77"
5 blocks	68"	85"	93½"
6 blocks	80"	100"	110"
7 blocks	92"	115"	126½"
8 blocks	104"	130"	
9 blocks	116"		
10 blocks	128"		

Bold entry in chart describes quilt as shown.

Bayberry & Holly

set sq	sash	set sq	sash	set sq	sash	set sq
sash	Bay-berry	sash	Bay-berry	sash	Bay-berry	sash
set sq	sash	set sq	sash	set sq	sash	set sq
sash	Bay-berry	sash	Bay-berry	sash	Bay-berry	sash
set sq	sash	set sq	sash	set sq	sash	set sq
sash	Bay-berry	sash	Bay-berry	sash	Bay-berry	sash
set sq	sash	set sq	sash	set sq	sash	set sq

Bayberry & Holly Quilt (page 85)
Finished Quilt Measurements, with Borders

Block Size:	10"	12"	14"
# Blocks per Row			
2 blocks	40"	48"	56"
3 blocks	**55"**	**66"**	**77"**
4 blocks	70"	84"	98"
5 blocks	85"	102"	119
6 blocks	100"	120"	
7 blocks	115"		
8 blocks	130"		
cut border	3"	3½"	4"

Bold entry in chart describes quilt as shown.

Christmas Goose

#48	Chain Edge Blk	#47	Chain Edge Blk	#48
Chain Edge Blk	Christmas Goose	Single Irish Chain	Christmas Goose	Chain Edge Blk
#47	Single Irish Chain	Christmas Goose	Single Irish Chain	#47
Chain Edge Blk	Christmas Goose	Single Irish Chain	Christmas Goose	Chain Edge Blk
#48	Chain Edge Blk	#47	Chain Edge Blk	#48

Christmas Goose Quilt (page 86)
Finished Quilt Measurements, with Borders

Block Size:	10"	12"	14"
# Blocks per Row*			
3 blocks	**50"**	**60"**	**70"**
5 blocks	70"	84"	98"
7 blocks	90"	108"	126"
9 blocks	110"	132"	
11 blocks	130"		

*denotes number of full-size blocks across or down the quilt center, excluding the #47 and #48 patches and chain edge blocks.

Bold entry in chart describes quilt as shown.

Santa Fe Sunset

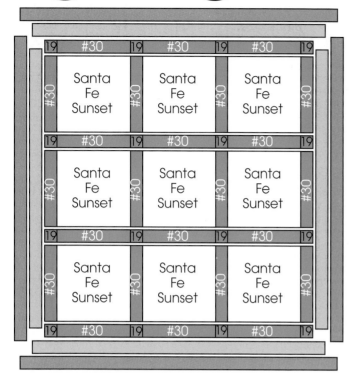

Santa Fe Sunset Quilt (page 87)
Finished Quilt Measurements, with Borders

Block Size:	10"	12"	14"
# Blocks per Row			
2 blocks	34"	38"	42"
3 blocks	**46"**	**52"**	**58"**
4 blocks	58"	66"	74"
5 blocks	70"	80"	90"
6 blocks	82"	94"	106"
7 blocks	94"	108"	122"
8 blocks	106"	122"	
9 blocks	118"		
cut borders	2½"	2½"	2½"
	2½"	2½"	2½"

Bold entry in chart describes quilt as shown.

Over the River

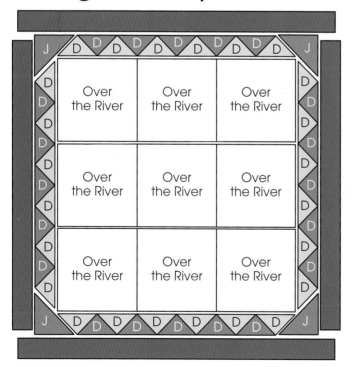

Over the River Quilt (page 88)
Finished Quilt Measurements, with Borders

Block Size:	12"	14"	15"
# Blocks per Row			
2 blocks	36"	42"	45"
3 blocks	**48"**	**56"**	**60"**
4 blocks	60"	70"	75"
5 blocks	72"	84"	90"
6 blocks	84"	98"	105"
7 blocks	96"	112"	120"
8 blocks	108"	126"	
9 blocks	120"		
10 blocks	132"		
cut border	3½"	4"	4¼"

Bold entry in chart describes quilt as shown.

Holiday Cheer

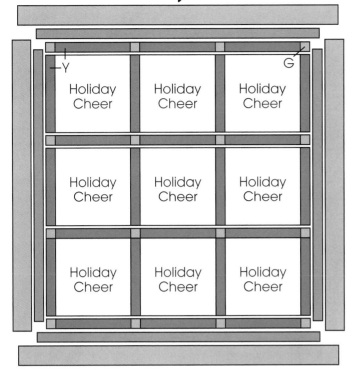

Holiday Cheer Quilt (page 89)
Finished Quilt Measurements, with Borders

Block Size:	12"	14"	15"
# Blocks per Row			
2 blocks	37½"	43¾"	46⅞"
3 blocks	**51"**	**59½"**	**63¾"**
4 blocks	64½"	75¼"	80⅝"
5 blocks	78"	91"	97½"
6 blocks	91½"	106¾"	114⅜"
7 blocks	105"	122½"	
8 blocks	118½"		
cut borders	2"	2¼"	2⅜"
	3½"	4"	4¼"

Bold entry in chart describes quilt as shown.

Kansas Summer

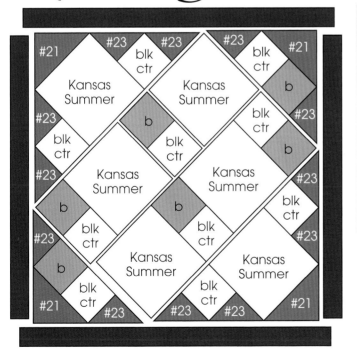

Kansas Summer Quilt (page 90)
Finished Quilt Measurements, with Borders

Block Size:	12"	15"	18"
# Blocks per Row*			
2½ blocks	**48½"**	**60½"**	**72⅝"**
3½ blocks	65⅜"	81¾"	98⅛"
4½ blocks	82⅜"	103"	123½"
5½ blocks	99⅜"	124¼"	
6½ blocks	116⅜"		
cut border	3½"	4¼"	5"

*denotes number of large blocks (or equivalent distance) across or down the quilt, with small blocks covering half the distance of large blocks

Bold entry in chart describes quilt as shown.

Wimbledon Star

Bold entry in chart describes quilt as shown.

Wimbledon Star Quilt (page 92)
Finished Quilt Measurements, with Borders

Block Size:	14"	15"	18"
# Blocks per Row*			
3 blocks	**49"**	**52½"**	**63"**
4 blocks	63"	67½"	81"
4½ blocks	70"	75"	90"
5 blocks	77"	82½"	99"
6 blocks	91"	97½"	117"
7 blocks	105"	112½"	135"
7½ blocks	112"	120"	
8 blocks	119"	127½"	
9 blocks	133"		
cut border	2¼"	2⅜"	2¾"

*denotes number of large blocks (or equivalent distance) across or down the quilt, with small blocks covering half the distance of large blocks

Tea for Two

Tea for Two Quilt (page 95)
Finished Quilt Measurements, with Borders

Block Size:	10"	15"	20"
# Blocks per Row			
2 blocks	33"	49½"	66"
3 blocks	**46"**	**69"**	**92"**
4 blocks	59"	88½"	118"
5 blocks	72"	108"	
6 blocks	85"	127½"	
7 blocks	98"		
8 blocks	111"		
9 blocks	124"		
cut border	1½"	2"	2½"

Bold entry in chart describes quilt as shown.

General Quilt Planning Charts

Use the charts below to help you plan your quilt dimensions. Mattress depth varies so much now that it is a good idea to measure.

Example: Your queen mattress is 9" deep. You want to use your quilt with a dust ruffle. In the third

chart, follow the yellow line for dust ruffles to the right to the blue column for queen size. Where row and column meet (green), find your ideal quilt size: 84" x 93". Use borders and the optional pillow tuck to make your blocks fit your ideal quilt size.

Mattress Sizes

	Twin	X-Long Twin	Double	Queen	King	Calif. King
mattress width x length	39" x 75"	39" x 80"	54" x 75"	60" x 80"	78" x 80"	72" x 84"
trad'l mattress depth	7"–9"	7"–9"	7"–9"	7"–9"	7"–9"	7"–9"
luxury mattress depth	13½"–22"	13½"–22"	13½"–22"	13½"–22"	13½"–22"	13½"–22"
box spring depth	9"	9"	9"	9"	9"	9"
low-profile bx spg depth	4½"	4½"	4½"	4½"	4½"	4½"

Standard Commercial Bedding Sizes

	Baby	Throw	Twin	Double	Queen	King
comforter	30" x 40"	40" x 50"	60" x 86"	86" x 86"	86" x 86"	102" x 86"
super-size comforter	36" x 40"	54" x 72"	70" x 90"	84" x 90"	90" x 96"	108" x 96"
coverlet	42" x 57"	60" x 80"	69" x 96"	84" x 96"	90" x 96"	108" x 96"
bedspread			80" x 108"	96" x 108"	102" x 118"	118" x 118"

Examples of Ideal Sizes for Bed Quilts*

Mattress 9" Deep, Box Springs 9" Deep

Drop	Twin	X-Long Twin	Double	Queen	King	Calif. King
to use with dust ruffle	63" x 88"	63" x 93"	78" x 88"	84" x 93"	102" x 93"	96" x 97"
to cover box springs	81" x 97"	81" x 102"	96" x 97"	102" x 102"	121" x 102"	115" x 107"

Mattress 15" Deep, Box Springs 9" Deep

Drop	Twin	X-Long Twin	Double	Queen	King	Calif. King
to use with dust ruffle	75" x 94"	75" x 99"	90" x 94"	96" x 99"	115" x 99"	109" x 104"
to cover box springs	93" x 104"	93" x 109"	109" x 104"	115" x 109"	133" x 109"	127" x 113"

Mattress 20" Deep, Box Springs 9" Deep

Drop	Twin	X-Long Twin	Double	Queen	King	Calif. King
to use with dust ruffle	85" x 99"	85" x 105"	100" x 99"	107" x 105"	125" x 105"	119" x 109"
to cover box springs	104" x 109"	104" x 114"	119" x 109"	125" x 114"	143" x 114"	137" x 118"

*Add 8"–18" to length for pillow tuck if desired. The pillow tuck and borders may be used to reconcile ideal size to some multiple of the block size in both length and width. All dimensions allow for 2% takeup (an estimate of the amount the quilt "shrinks" due to thickness).

These charts will save you time if you want to design your own quilts

Use the charts on these two pages to determine dimensions or block quantities for quilts of various arrangements. Also use them to find a setting that will give you the quilt size that you desire.

Example: You want to know dimensions for a quilt made from 12" blocks set diagonally with 4 blocks across and 5 blocks down. Follow the blue "diagonal, side by side" column of the 12" chart

Quilt Dimensions Using 5" Blocks

# blks per side	Straight Sets		Diagonal Sets	
	side by side	1¼" fin sashes	side by side	1¼" fin sashes
2	10"	13¾"	14⅛"	19½"
3	15"	20"	21¼"	28¼"
4	20"	26¼"	28¼"	37⅛"
5	25"	32½"	35⅜"	46"
6	30"	38¾"	42⅜"	54¾"
7	35"	45"	49½"	63⅝"
8	40"	51¼"	56⅝"	72½"
9	45"	57½"	63⅝"	81⅜"
10	50"	63¾"	70¾"	90⅛"
11	55"	70"	77¾"	99"
12	60"	76¼"	84⅞"	107⅞"
13	65"	82½"	91⅞"	116⅝"
14	70"	88¾"	99"	125½"
15	75"	95"	106⅛"	
16	80"	101¼"	113⅛"	
17	85"	107½"	120¼"	
18	90"	113¾"	127¼"	
19	95"	120"		
20	100"	126¼"		

Quilt Dimensions Using 6" Blocks

# blks per side	Straight Sets			Diagonal Sets		
	side by side	1½" fin sash	2" fin sash	side by side	1" fin sash	1½" fin sash
2	12"	16½"	18"	17"	21¼"	23⅜"
3	18"	24"	26"	25½"	31⅛"	34"
4	24"	31½"	34"	34"	41"	44½"
5	30"	39"	42"	42⅜"	50⅞"	55⅛"
6	36"	46½"	50"	50⅞"	60¾"	65¾"
7	42"	54"	58"	59⅜"	70¾"	76⅜"
8	48"	61½"	66"	67⅞"	80⅝"	87"
9	54"	69"	74"	76⅜"	90½"	97⅝"
10	60"	76½"	82"	84⅞"	100⅜"	108⅛"
11	66"	84"	90"	93⅜"	110¼"	118¾"
12	72"	91½"	98"	101⅞"	120¼"	129⅜"
13	78"	99"	106"	110¼"		
14	84"	106½"	114"	118¾"		
15	90"	114"	122"	127¼"		
16	96"	121½"				
17	102"	129"				
18	108"					
19	114"					

Quilt Dimensions Using 15" Blocks

# blks per side	Straight Sets			Diagonal Sets		
	side by side	with 2½" sash	with 3" sash	side by side	with 1½" sash	with 2½" sash
2	30"	37½"	39"	42⅜"	48¾"	53"
3	45"	55"	57"	63⅝"	72⅛"	77¾"
4	60"	72½"	75"	84⅞"	95½"	102½"
5	75"	90"	93"	106⅛"	118¾"	127¼"
6	90"	107½"	111"	127¼"		
7	105"	125"	129"			
8	120"					

Quilt Dimensions Using 14" Blocks

# blks per side	Straight Sets			Diagonal Sets		
	side by side	with 1¾" sash	with 3½" sash	side by side	with 1¾" sash	with 2" sash
2	28"	33¼"	38½"	39⅝"	47"	48⅛"
3	42"	49"	56"	59⅜"	69¼"	70¾"
4	56"	64¾"	73½"	79¼"	91⅝"	93⅜"
5	70"	80½"	91"	99"	113⅞"	116"
6	84"	96¼"	108½"	118¾"		
7	98"	112"	126"			
8	112"	127¾"				
9	126"					

down to the pink row for 4 blocks per side. Your quilt's width (67⅞") is listed in the purple area where row and column meet. Follow the same blue column down one more line to the yellow row for 5 blocks per side. Your quilt's length is 84⅞".
All dimensions on pgs. 114–115 are finished sizes.

Notes: Cut sashes ½" wider than the size listed. If your quilt needs rows of even or odd numbers for balance, take that into account. Borders are not included in these dimensions. If the quilt dimensions listed don't match your ideal quilt size, consider borders or a different set or block size.

Quilt Dimensions Using 8" Blocks

# blks per side	Straight Sets			Diagonal Sets		
	side by side	1" fin sash	2" fin sash	side by side	1" fin sash	2" fin sash
2	16"	19"	22"	22⅝"	26⅞"	31⅛"
3	24"	28"	32"	34"	39⅝"	45¼"
4	32"	37"	42"	45¼"	52⅜"	59⅜"
5	40"	46"	52"	56⅝"	65"	73½"
6	48"	55"	62"	67⅞"	77¾"	87⅝"
7	56"	64"	72"	79¼"	90½"	101⅞"
8	64"	73"	82"	90½"	103¼"	116"
9	72"	82"	92"	101⅞"	116"	
10	80"	91"	102"	113⅛"	128¾"	
11	88"	100"	112"	124½"		
12	96"	109"	122"			
13	104"	118"				
14	112"					
15	120"					

Quilt Dimensions Using 9" Blocks

# blks per side	Straight Sets			Diagonal Sets		
	side by side	1½" fin sash	3" fin sash	side by side	1⅛" fin sash	1½" fin sash
2	18"	22½"	27"	25½"	30¼"	31⅞"
3	27"	33"	39"	38⅛"	44½"	46⅝"
4	36"	43½"	51"	50⅞"	58⅞"	61½"
5	45"	54"	63"	63⅝"	73⅛"	76⅜"
6	54"	64½"	75"	76⅜"	87½"	91¼"
7	63"	75"	87"	89⅛"	101⅞"	106⅛"
8	72"	85½"	99"	101⅞"	116⅛"	120⅞"
9	81"	96"	111"	114½"		
10	90"	106½"	123"	127¼"		
11	99"	117"				
12	108"	127½"				
13	117"					
14	126"					

Quilt Dimensions Using 12" Blocks

# blks per side	Straight Sets			Diagonal Sets		
	side by side	1½" fin sash	3" fin sash	side by side	1½" fin sash	3" fin sash
2	24"	28½"	33"	34"	40¼"	46⅝"
3	36"	42"	48"	50⅞"	59⅜"	67⅞"
4	48"	55½"	63"	67⅞"	78½"	89⅛"
5	60"	69"	78"	84⅞"	97⅝"	110¼"
6	72"	82½"	93"	101⅞"	116⅝"	
7	84"	96"	108"	118¾"		
8	96"	109½"	123"			
9	108"	123"	138"			
10	120"					

Quilt Dimensions Using 10" Blocks

# blks per side	Straight Sets			Diagonal Sets		
	side by side	2" fin sash	2½" fin sash	side by side	1¼" fin sash	2" fin sash
2	20"	26"	27½"	28¼"	33⅝"	36¾"
3	30"	38"	40"	42⅜"	49½"	53¾"
4	40"	50"	52½"	56⅝"	65⅜"	70¾"
5	50"	62"	65"	70¾"	81⅜"	87⅝"
6	60"	74"	77½"	84⅞"	97¼"	104⅝"
7	70"	86"	90"	99"	113⅛"	121⅝"
8	80"	98"	102½"	113⅛"	129"	
9	90"	110"	115"	127¼"		
10	100"	122"	127½"			
11	110"					
12	120"					

These charts will save you time if you want to design your own quilts

Use the charts below to determine the number of blocks, alternate blocks, edge triangles, sashes, and setting squares your diagonally-set quilt requires.

Example: Your quilt has 5 blocks across and 6 blocks down. Your quilt is set with alternate plain squares. Follow the pink-highlighted row for 5 x 6 blocks to the right to the column headed in blue, #main blocks. The purple rectangle where row and column meet indicates that your quilt has 30 main blocks. Continue to the right to the yellow space in the last column. Your quilt also has 20 alternate blocks.

Terms Defined: *across and down:* count blocks in the horizontal and vertical rows you see, not in the diagonal rows you sew. *Total number of blocks:* includes blocks as well as alternate blocks for sets that have them. *Edge triangles:* the large triangles that square off the quilt around the edges. *Setting squares:* the small squares where sashes intersect. *Sashes:* the block-length strips that separate blocks from one another. *Setting triangles:* triangles that finish half the size of a setting square; these are sometimes used instead of setting squares around the edges of a quilt. In such a case, setting squares are still used in the interior. *Main blocks:* the pieced or appliquéd blocks of the most abundant type in the quilt. *Alternate Blocks:* plain squares or contrasting blocks that are placed between main blocks.

Diagonal Sets: Number of Blocks & Setting Patches Required

number of blocks across and down	total number of blocks	# of edge trian-gles	if quilt has sashes number of setting squares	number of sashes	if edge setting squares are halved # setting squares	#setting triangles	if quilt has alternate blocks #main blocks	# alt blocks
2 x 2	5	4	12	16	4	8	4	1
2 x 3	8	6	17	24	7	10	6	2
2 x 4	11	8	22	32	10	12	8	3
3 x 3	13	8	24	36	12	12	9	4
3 x 4	18	10	31	48	17	14	12	6
4 x 4	25	12	40	64	24	16	16	9
4 x 5	32	14	49	80	31	18	20	12
4 x 6	39	16	58	96	38	20	24	15
5 x 5	41	16	60	100	40	20	25	16
5 x 6	50	18	71	120	49	22	30	20
5 x 7	59	20	82	140	58	24	35	24
6 x 6	61	20	84	144	60	24	36	25
6 x 7	72	22	97	168	71	26	42	30
6 x 8	83	24	110	192	82	28	48	35
7 x 7	85	24	112	196	84	28	49	36
7 x 8	98	26	127	224	97	30	56	42
7 x 9	111	28	142	252	110	32	63	48
8 x 8	113	28	144	256	112	32	64	49
8 x 9	128	30	161	288	127	34	72	56
8 x 10	143	32	178	320	142	36	80	63
8 x 11	158	34	195	352	157	38	88	70
9 x 9	145	32	180	324	144	36	81	64
9 x 10	162	34	199	360	161	38	90	72
9 x 11	179	36	218	396	178	40	99	80
9 x 12	196	38	237	432	195	42	108	88

Diagonal Sets: Number of Blocks & Setting Patches Required, continued

number of blocks across and down	total number of blocks	# of edge trian-gles	if quilt has sashes number of setting squares	number of sashes	if edge setting squares are halved # setting squares	#setting triangles	if quilt has alternate blocks #main blocks	# alt blocks
10 x 10	181	36	220	400	180	40	100	81
10 x 11	200	38	241	440	199	42	110	90
10 x 12	219	40	262	480	218	44	120	99
10 x 13	238	42	283	520	237	46	130	108
11 x 11	221	40	264	484	220	44	121	100
11 x 12	242	42	287	528	241	46	132	110
11 x 13	263	44	310	572	262	48	143	120
11 x 14	284	46	333	616	283	50	154	130
11 x 15	305	48	356	660	304	52	165	140
12 x 12	265	44	312	576	264	48	144	121
12 x 13	288	46	337	624	287	50	156	132
12 x 14	311	48	362	672	310	52	168	143
12 x 15	334	50	387	720	333	54	180	154
12 x 16	357	52	412	768	356	56	192	165
13 x 13	313	48	364	676	312	52	169	144
13 x 14	338	50	391	728	337	54	182	156
13 x 15	363	52	418	780	362	56	195	168
13 x 16	388	54	445	832	387	58	208	180
13 x 17	413	56	472	884	412	60	221	192
14 x 14	365	52	420	784	364	56	196	169
14 x 15	392	54	449	840	391	58	210	182
14 x 16	419	56	478	896	418	60	224	195
14 x 17	446	58	507	952	445	62	238	208
14 x 18	473	60	536	1008	472	64	252	221
15 x 15	421	56	480	900	420	60	225	196
15 x 16	450	58	511	960	449	62	240	210
15 x 17	479	60	542	1020	478	64	255	224
15 x 18	508	62	573	1080	507	66	270	238
16 x 16	481	60	544	1024	480	64	256	225
16 x 17	512	62	577	1088	511	66	272	240
16 x 18	543	64	610	1152	542	68	288	255
17 x 17	545	64	612	1156	544	68	289	256
17 x 18	578	66	647	1224	577	70	306	272
18 x 18	613	68	684	1296	612	72	324	289

These charts will save you time if you want to design your own quilts

Use the charts on these two pages to find the number of blocks, sashes, setting squares, or alternate blocks needed for a quilt having horizontal and vertical rows. The "all sets" column tells the block quantity for quilts with side-by-side blocks or sashing. It also tells the combined totals of main and alternate blocks. "Inside" sashes are between blocks; "outside" sashes are around the edges.

Example: Your quilt has 3 x 5 blocks with alternate plain squares. Follow the 3 x 5 row from the left to the last two columns on the right. There you will find your number of blocks, 8, and alternate blocks, 7. *(**Entries in bold type are balanced sets with all four corners matching.**)*

Straight Sets: Number of Blocks & Setting Patches Required

# blocks across and down	all sets total # of blocks	if quilt has sashes inside & outside number of setting squares	number of sashes	if quilt has sashes inside only number setting squares	number of sashes	if quilt has alternate blocks number of main blocks	number alternate blocks
2 x 2	4	9	12	1	4	2	2
2 x 3	6	12	17	2	7	3	3
3 x 3	9	16	24	4	12	**5**	**4**
3 x 4	12	20	31	6	17	6	6
3 x 5	15	24	38	8	22	**8**	**7**
4 x 4	16	25	40	9	24	8	8
4 x 5	20	30	49	12	31	10	10
4 x 6	24	35	58	15	38	12	12
5 x 5	25	36	60	16	40	**13**	**12**
5 x 6	30	42	71	20	49	15	15
5 x 7	35	48	82	24	58	**18**	**17**
6 x 6	36	49	84	25	60	18	18
6 x 7	42	56	97	30	71	21	21
6 x 8	48	63	110	35	82	24	24
7 x 7	49	64	112	36	84	**25**	**24**
7 x 8	56	72	127	42	97	28	28
7 x 9	63	80	142	48	110	**32**	**31**
8 x 8	64	81	144	49	112	32	32
8 x 9	72	90	161	56	127	36	36
8 x 10	80	99	178	63	142	40	40
8 x 11	88	108	195	70	157	44	44
9 x 9	81	100	180	64	144	**41**	**40**
9 x 10	90	110	199	72	161	45	45
9 x 11	99	120	218	80	178	**50**	**49**
9 x 12	108	130	237	88	195	54	54
10 x 10	100	121	220	81	180	50	50
10 x 11	110	132	241	90	199	55	55
10 x 12	120	143	262	99	218	60	60
10 x 13	130	154	283	108	237	65	65

Straight Sets: Number of Blocks & Setting Patches Required, continued

# blocks across and down	all sets total # of blocks	if quilt has sashes inside & outside		if quilt has sashes inside only		if quilt has alternate blocks	
		number of setting squares	number of sashes	number setting squares	number of sashes	number of main blocks	number alternate blocks
11 x 11	121	144	264	100	220	**61**	**60**
11 x 12	132	156	287	110	241	66	66
11 x 13	143	168	310	120	262	**72**	**71**
11 x 14	154	180	333	130	283	77	77
12 x 12	144	169	312	121	264	72	72
12 x 13	156	182	337	132	287	78	78
12 x 14	168	195	362	143	310	84	84
12 x 15	180	208	387	154	333	90	90
12 x 16	192	221	412	165	356	96	96
13 x 13	169	196	364	144	312	**85**	**84**
13 x 14	182	210	391	156	337	91	91
13 x 15	195	224	418	168	362	**98**	**97**
13 x 16	208	238	445	180	387	104	104
13 x 17	221	252	472	192	412	**111**	**110**
14 x 14	196	225	420	169	364	98	98
14 x 15	210	240	449	182	391	105	105
14 x 16	224	255	478	195	418	112	112
14 x 17	238	270	507	208	445	119	119
14 x 18	252	285	536	221	472	126	126
15 x 15	225	256	480	196	420	**113**	**112**
15 x 16	240	272	511	210	449	120	120
15 x 17	255	288	542	224	478	**128**	**127**
15 x 18	270	304	573	238	507	135	135
15 x 19	285	320	604	252	536	**143**	**142**
16 x 16	256	289	544	225	480	128	128
16 x 17	272	306	577	240	511	136	136
16 x 18	288	323	610	255	542	144	144
16 x 19	304	340	643	270	573	152	152
16 x 20	320	357	676	285	604	160	160
17 x 17	289	324	612	256	544	**145**	**144**
17 x 18	306	342	647	272	577	153	153
17 x 19	323	360	682	288	610	**162**	**161**
17 x 20	340	378	717	304	643	170	170
17 x 21	357	396	752	320	676	**179**	**178**

These charts will save you time if you want to design your own quilts

The next three charts list yardage for sashes, alternate blocks, and edge triangles.

Example: Your quilt has 12" blocks set with 49 sashes that finish 2" wide. In the chart below, follow the row for 12" blocks and 2" sashes to the right to

the first number larger than 49, in this case, 64. Follow that column to the top to determine that you need 1½ yds. to cut up to 64 sashes. *Yardages are for 42"-wide fabric and allow for 5% shrinkage. In some cases you will have a little fabric left over.*

Number of Sashes You Can Cut from Various Yardages

fin blk size	fin sash width	cut sash dimensions	# in ½ yd	# in 1 yd	# in 1½ yds	# in 2 yds	# in 2½ yds	# in 3 yds	# in 3½ yds	# in 4 yds	# in 4½ yds	# in 5 yds
5"	1"	1½" x 5½"	78	156	234	312	390	468	546	624	728	806
5"	1¼"	1¾" x 5½"	66	132	198	264	330	396	462	528	616	682
6"	1"	1½" x 6½"	52	130	182	260	338	390	468	546	598	676
6"	1½"	2" x 6½"	40	100	140	200	260	300	360	420	460	520
6"	2"	2½" x 6½"	32	80	112	160	208	240	288	336	368	416
7"	⅞"	1⅜" x 7½"	58	116	174	261	319	377	435	522	580	638
7"	1¾"	2¼" x 7½"	34	68	102	153	187	221	255	306	340	374
7½"	1¼"	1¾" x 8"	44	88	132	176	220	264	308	374	418	462
7½"	1⅞"	2⅜" x 8"	32	64	96	128	160	192	224	272	304	336
8"	1"	1½" x 8½"	52	104	156	208	260	312	364	416	468	520
8"	1¾"	2¼" x 8½"	34	68	102	136	170	204	238	272	306	340
8"	2"	2½" x 8½"	32	64	96	128	160	192	224	256	288	320
9"	1⅛"	1⅝" x 9½"	24	72	120	168	216	240	288	336	384	432
9"	1½"	2" x 9½"	20	60	100	140	180	200	240	280	320	360
9"	2"	2½" x 9½"	16	48	80	112	144	160	192	224	256	288
9"	2¼"	2¾" x 9½"	14	42	70	98	126	140	168	196	224	252
9"	3"	3½" x 9½"	11	33	55	77	99	110	132	154	176	198
10"	1¼"	1¾" x 10½"	22	66	88	132	176	198	242	286	308	352
10"	2"	2½" x 10½"	16	48	64	96	128	144	176	208	224	256
10"	2½"	3" x 10½"	13	39	52	78	104	117	143	169	182	208
12"	1½"	2" x 12½"	20	40	80	100	120	160	180	200	240	260
12"	2"	2½" x 12½"	16	32	64	80	96	128	144	160	192	208
12"	2½"	3" x 12½"	13	26	52	65	78	104	117	130	156	169
12"	3"	3½" x 12½"	11	22	44	55	66	88	99	110	132	143
12"	4"	4½" x 12½"	8	16	32	40	48	64	72	80	96	104
14"	1¾"	2¼" x 14½"	17	34	51	68	85	119	136	153	170	187
14"	2"	2½" x 14½"	16	32	48	64	80	112	128	144	160	176
14"	3"	3½" x 14½"	11	22	33	44	55	77	88	99	110	121
14"	3½"	4" x 14½"	10	20	30	40	50	70	80	90	100	110
15"	1½"	2" x 15½"	20	40	60	80	100	120	140	160	180	220

Number of Sashes You Can Cut from Various Yardages, continued

fin blk size	fin sash width	cut sash dimensions	# in ½ yd	# in 1 yd	# in 1½ yds	# in 2 yds	# in 2½ yds	# in 3 yds	# in 3½ yds	# in 4 yds	# in 4½ yds	# in 5 yds
15"	1⅞"	2⅜" x 15½"	16	32	48	64	80	96	112	128	144	176
15"	2½"	3" x 15½"	13	26	39	52	65	78	91	104	117	143
15"	3"	3½" x 15½"	11	22	33	44	55	66	77	88	99	121
15"	5"	5½" x 15½"	7	14	21	28	35	42	49	56	63	77
18"	2¼"	2¾" x 18½"		14	28	42	56	70	84	98	112	126
18"	4½"	5" x 18½"		8	16	24	32	40	48	56	64	72
20"	2"	2½" x 20½"		16	32	48	64	80	80	96	112	128
20"	2½"	3" x 20½"		13	26	39	52	65	65	78	91	104
20"	4"	4½" x 20½"		8	16	24	32	40	40	48	56	64

Number of Alternate Plain Squares You Can Cut from Various Yardages

fin blk size	5"	6"	7"	7½"	8"	9"	10"	12"	14"	15"	18"	20"
cut square	5½"	6½"	7½"	8"	8½"	9½"	10½"	12½"	14½"	15½"	18½"	20½"
yardage												
# in ½ yd	21	12	10	10	8	4	3	3	2	2		
# in ⅝ yd		18				8	6				2	1
# in ¾ yd	28		15	15	12			6				
# in ⅞ yd	35	24				12	6		4			
# in 1 yd	42	30	20	20	16		9			4		
# in 1¼ yds	49	36	25	25	20	16	12	9			4	2
# in 1½ yds	63	42	30	30	24	20		12	6	6		
# in 1¾ yds	70	54	35	35	28	24	15		8		6	
# in 2 yds	84	60	45	40	32	28	18	15		8		3
# in 2¼ yds	98	66	50	45	36	32	21	18	10		8	
# in 2½ yds	105	78	55	50	40	36	24			10		4
# in 2¾ yds	119	84	60	55	44			21	12	12	10	
# in 3 yds	126	90	65	60	48	40	27	24	14			5
# in 3½ yds	147	108	75	70	56	48	33	27	16	14	12	
# in 4 yds	168	126	90	85	64	56	39	30	18	16	14	6
# in 4½ yds	196	138	100	95	72	64	42	36	20	18	16	7
# in 5 yds	217	156	110	105	80	72	48	39	22	22	18	8
# in 5½ yds	238	174	125	115	88	76	51	45	26	24	20	9
# in 6 yds	259	186	135	125	96	84	57	48	28	26	22	10
# in 6½ yds	280	204	145	135	104	92	63	51	30	28	24	
# in 7 yds	301	216	155	145	112	100	66	57	32	30		11

These charts will save you time if you want to design your own quilts

fin. blk. size	5"	6"	7"	7½"	8"	9"	10"	12"	14"	15"	18"	20"
cut square	8¼+"	9¾"	11⅛"	11⅞"	12½"	13⅞+"	15⅜"	18¼"	21"	22⅜+"	26⅝+"	29½"
yardage												
½ yd	32	16	12	12	12	8	8					
⅝ yd		32						8	4			
¾ yd	48		24	24	24					4		
⅞ yd		48				16					4	4
1 yd	64		36				16					
1¼ yds	80	64		36	36	24		16	8			
1½ yds			48	48	48		24			8		
1¾ yds						32		24			8	8
2 yds						32			12	12		
2½ yds							32		16		12	
2¾ yds										16		12
3¼ yds									20		16	

The chart below lists yardages for quilt backs.

Example: Your quilt measures 86" x 94". That means your quilt's width (86") is between 75" and 113", so use the yellow section. Find 94" or the next larger number in the "quilt length" column. Follow the line (95") to the left in the same section to find the yardage required, in this case, 8¾ yds.

If you don't mind crosswise seams on the back, you can switch length and width and buy less fabric. For your 86" x 94" quilt, use the yellow section for a 94" quilt width (your length). Look up your quilt's width, 86", in the length column. This requires 8 yds. rather than the 8¾ yds. required for lengthwise seams.

Figures are based on 42" fabric width and allow 5% for shrinkage and 5" extra length and width.

Yardage for Quilt Backings

1 panel (seamless) quilts to 35" wide		2 panels (1 seam) quilts 36"–74" wide		2 panels, cont'd quilts 36"–74" wide		3 panels (2 seams) quilts 75"–113" wide		3 panels, cont'd quilts 75"–113" wide	
ydg	fin quilt length	ydg	fin quilt length	ydg	fin quilt length	ydg	fin quilt length	ydg	fin quilt length
1¼ yds	37"	2½ yds	37"	4½ yds	72"	7 yds	75"	10 yds	109"
1½ yds	46"	2¾ yds	42"	4¾ yds	76"	7¼ yds	77"	10¼ yds	112"
		3 yds	46"	5 yds	80"	7½ yds	80"	10½ yds	115"
		3¼ yds	50"	5¼ yds	85"	7¾ yds	83"	10¾ yds	117"
		3½ yds	55"	5½ yds	89"	8 yds	86"	11 yds	120"
		3¾ yds	59"	5¾ yds	93"	8¼ yds	89"	11¼ yds	123"
		4 yds	63"	6 yds	97"	8½ yds	92"	11½ yds	126"
		4¼ yds	67"			8¾ yds	95"	11¾ yds	129"
						9 yds	97"	12 yds	132"
						9¼ yds	100"	12¼ yds	135"
						9½ yds	103"	12½ yds	137"
						9¾ yds	106"	12¾ yds	140"

These charts will save you time if you want to design your own quilts

Use the chart below to determine how much binding fabric to buy.

Example: Your quilt measures 86" x 94", and you plan to use double binding cut on the bias. The green area lists your binding type. Your quilt size is in the 111" x 111" range; follow that row left; you need ¾ yd.

Yardage for Quilt Bindings

Straight Grain Binding doubled, cut 2" wide		Straight Grain Binding single, cut 1¼" wide		Bias Binding doubled, cut 2" wide		Bias Binding single, cut 1¼" wide	
ydg	quilt size	ydg	quilt size	ydg	quilt size	ydg	quilt size
½ yd	to 81" x 81" or 72" x 90"	½ yd	to 131" x 131" or 145" x 116"	½ yd	to 70" x 70" or 60" x 80"	½ yd	to 111" x 111" or 108" x 114"
¾ yd	to 124" x 124" or 134" x 114"	¾ yd	larger size	¾ yd	to 111" x 111" or 108" x 114"	¾ yd	larger size
1 yd	larger size			1 yd	larger size		

Yardage Charts for Block Patches

Use the charts on pages 123–125 to determine yardage for your quilt. Because these charts are based on 1 yard, some patch quantities will require slightly more or less yardage than the chart figures indicate. *Always allow enough extra to cut a row of the largest patches. For patches up to about 4¼", ⅛ yard extra will do; for patches up to 8½", ¼ yard extra will do.*

First count how many patches of each size and shape your quilt requires. Use the chart for your patch shape. Add together all of the yardages for patches to be cut from the same fabric.

Example 1A: Suppose your quilt requires 420 red squares cut 2" and 210 red half-square triangles cut 2⅞". Start with the squares. Find 2" on the left of the squares chart. Follow that row to the right to see that you can cut 340 squares of this size from 1 yd. of fabric. Divide the 420 (your number) by 340

(number per yd.). The result is 1.235. The Fractions & Decimal Equivalents chart below left will translate that figure to about 1¼ yds. Add at least ⅛ yard extra, for a total of 1⅜ yds. The extra isn't optional. If you don't add it, you could end up with a row of half squares instead of half a row of squares.

Next, figure yardage for the red triangles (next page).

Fractions & Decimal Equivalents

fraction	decimal	fraction	decimal
¹⁄₁₆	.0625	½+	.5625
⅛	.125	⅝	.625
⅛+	.1875	⅝+	.6875
¼	.25	¾	.75
¼+	.3125	¾+	.8125
⅜	.375	⅞	.875
⅜+	.4375	⅞+	.9375
½	.5		

Number of Squares You Can Cut from 1 Yard of Fabric

Cut Size of Square	Number per Yard	Cut Size of Square (continued)	Number per Yard	Cut Size of Square (continued)	Number per Yard
1"	1360	2¼"	255	4½"	56
1⅛"	1050	2⅜"	224	4¾"	56
1¼"	864	2½"	208	5"	48
1¼+"	780	2⅝"	195	5½"	42
1⅜"	696	2¾"	168	5¾"	30
1⅜+"	621	2⅞"	143	6⅛"	30
1½"	572	3"	143	6½"	30
1½+"	525	3⅛"	120	7½"	20
1⅝"	504	3¼+"	120	8"	20
1⅝+"	460	3½"	99	8½"	16
1¾"	418	3⅝+"	90	9½"	12
1¾+"	396	3⅞"	80	10½"	9
1⅞+"	340	4"	80	12½"	6
2"	340	4+"	72	15½"	4
2⅛+"	270	4¼"	72		

+ indicates number halfway between listed size & next higher eighth inch.

To figure yardage for triangles that are cut two to a square, use the pink-bordered chart below.

Example 1B: To continue the example from page 123, find 2⅞" on the left. Follow that row to the right; you can cut 286 triangles of this size from one yard. Divide 210 (your number) by 286. You need 0.73 yd. or ¾ yd. Adding at least ⅛ yd. to be safe, you get ⅞ yd.

Finally, add to the red triangle yardage the 1⅜ yd. for the red squares for a total of 2¼ yds. of red fabric.

To figure yardage for triangles that are cut four to a square, use the blue-bordered chart below.

Example 2: Another quilt requires 200 green quarter-square triangles cut 4¼". Find 4¼" on the left of the 1st section of the blue chart below. Follow that row to the right to see that you can cut 288 of these triangles per yd. Divide 200 (your number) by 288. The result is 0.69 or a little over ⅝ yd. Adding at least ⅛ yard extra, you get a little more than ¾ yd.; buy ⅞ yd. to be safe.

Number of Triangles (Half-Square) You Can Cut from 1 Yard of Fabric

Cut Size of Patches	Number per Yard	(continued) Cut Size of Patches	Number per Yard
1½"	1144	4⅝"	112
1½+"	1050	4⅞"	112
1⅝"	1008	5⅛"	84
1⅝+"	920	5⅜"	84
1¾"	836	5¾+"	60
1⅞"	756	5⅞"	60
1⅞+"	680	6⅛"	60
2"	680	6⅛+"	60
2+"	608	6½"	60
2⅛"	576	6⅞"	40
2¼"	510	7¼"	40
2⅜"	448	7⅝"	40
2⅜+"	448	7⅞"	40
2⅝"	390	7⅞+"	40
2¾"	336	8⅜"	32
2⅞"	286	8⅞"	24
3"	286	9⅜"	24
3⅛"	240	9⅞"	24
3⅜"	220	10⅞"	18
3½"	198	11⅜"	18
3⅝+"	180	11⅜+"	12
3⅞"	160	12⅛"	12
4+"	144	13½+"	8
4¼"	144	17⅞"	4
4⅜"	126	22+"	2

Number of Triangles (Quarter-Square) You Can Cut from 1 Yard of Fabric

Cut Size of Patches	Number per Yard	(continued) Cut Size of Patches	Number per Yard
2"	1360	6¼"	120
2⅛"	1152	6½"	120
2¼"	1020	6½+"	120
2⅜"	896	6⅞"	80
2½"	832	7¼"	80
2⅝"	780	7⅝"	80
2¾"	672	8"	80
2⅞"	572	8¼"	64
3"	572	8¼+"	64
3⅛"	480	8¾"	48
3¼"	480	9¼"	48
3⅜"	440	9¾"	48
3½"	396	10¼"	36
3⅝+"	360	11⅛"	36
3¾"	360	11¼"	36
3⅞"	320	11¾"	24
4+"	288	11¾+"	24
4¼"	288	12½"	24
4⅜+"	252	13¼"	24
4⅝"	224	13⅞+"	16
4¾"	224	14"	16
5"	192	15¼"	16
5¼"	168	15⅜"	16
5½"	168	16¼"	16
5¾"	120	18¼"	8
6⅛+"	120	22⅜+"	4

+ indicates a number halfway between the listed size and the next higher eighth inch.
Yardage figures are based on 42" fabric width and allow for 5% shrinkage.
Always add at least the size of the largest patch to be on the safe side.

Use the chart below to figure yardage for rectangles.

Example 3: Your quilt requires 30 blue rectangles cut 2" wide and 6½" long. Find 2" x 6½" on the left of the 2nd section of the rectangles chart below. Follow that row to the right to see that you can cut 100 rectangles of this size from 1 yd. of fabric. Divide the 30 (your number) by 100 (number per yd.). The result is 0.3 or about ⅜ yd. Buy ½ yd. just to be safe.

Number of Rectangles You Can Cut from 1 Yard of Fabric

Cut Size of Patch	Number per Yard	(continued) Cut Size of Patch	Number per Yard	(continued) Cut Size of Patch	Number per Yard	(continued) Cut Size of Patch	Number per Yard
1" x 1½"	880	1¾" x 2½"	286	2⅜" x 15½"	32	3½" x 8½"	44
1" x 2¼"	600	1¾" x 3"	242	2½" x 3"	176	3½" x 9½"	33
1" x 2½"	520	1¾" x 4¼"	176	2½" x 3½"	144	3½" x 12½"	22
1" x 8½"	160	1¾" x 5"	132	2½" x 4½"	112	3½" x 14"	22
1" x 9½"	120	1¾" x 5½"	132	2½" x 5½"	96	3½" x 14½"	22
1⅛" x 1¾"	665	1¾" x 6¾"	110	2½" x 6½"	80	3½" x 15½"	22
1¼" x 2"	544	1¾" x 7½"	88	2½" x 8½"	64	3½" x 18½"	11
1¼" x 3½"	288	1¾" x 8"	88	2½" x 9½"	48	4" x 7½"	40
1¼" x 6½"	160	1¾" x 10½"	66	2½" x 10½"	48	4" x 11"	30
1⅜" x 1½"	638	2" x 2½"	260	2½" x 12½"	32	4" x 14½"	20
1⅜" x 2¼"	435	2" x 3½"	180	2½" x 14½"	32	4¼" x 8"	36
1⅜" x 3¼"	290	2" x 4¼"	160	2½" x 20½"	16	4¼" x 11¾"	18
1⅜" x 5"	174	2" x 5"	120	2¾" x 5"	84	4¼" x 15½"	18
1⅜+" x 2⅜"	378	2" x 5½"	120	2¾" x 7¼"	56	4½" x 8½"	32
1⅜+" x 4¼"	216	2" x 6½"	100	2¾" x 9½"	42	4½" x 12½"	16
1½" x 2¼"	390	2" x 8"	80	2¾" x 18½"	14	4½" x 20½"	8
1½" x 2½"	338	2" x 8½"	80	3" x 5"	78	4½" x 24½"	8
1½" x 3"	286	2" x 9½"	60	3" x 5½"	78	5" x 8½"	32
1½" x 3½"	234	2" x 11"	60	3" x 7½"	52	5" x 9½"	24
1½" x 4"	208	2" x 12½"	40	3" x 8"	52	5½" x 9½"	21
1½" x 4½"	182	2" x 15½"	40	3" x 10½"	39	5½" x 10½"	21
1½" x 5½"	156	2¼" x 3¼"	170	3" x 12½"	26	6½" x 9½"	18
1½" x 6½"	130	2¼" x 4"	136	3" x 13"	26	6½" x 10½"	18
1½" x 8½"	104	2¼" x 5"	102	3" x 14½"	26	6½" x 12½"	12
1½" x 9½"	78	2¼" x 5¾"	85	3" x 15½"	26	6½" x 15½"	12
1½" x 10½"	78	2¼" x 7½"	68	3" x 17"	26	7½" x 12½"	10
1½" x 12½"	52	2¼" x 8½"	68	3" x 20½"	13	7½" x 14½"	10
1½" x 14½"	52	2¼" x 9¼"	51	3" x 25½"	13	8" x 15½"	10
1⅝" x 2¾"	288	2¼" x 14½"	34	3¼" x 6"	60	8½" x 14½"	8
1⅝" x 5"	144	2⅜" x 4¼"	128	3½" x 5½"	66	9½" x 15½"	8
1⅝" x 6⅛"	120	2⅜" x 8"	64	3½" x 6½"	55	12½" x 20½"	3
1⅝" x 9½"	72	2⅜" x 9⅞"	48				

+ indicates a number halfway between the listed size and the next higher eighth inch.

These charts will save you time if you want to design your own quilts

Block Pattern Index

Quilt Pattern Index

Chart Index

Other Books by Judy Martin